A History of Gower

A History of Gower

by
Derek Draisey

Logaston Press

LOGASTON PRESS
Little Logaston, Woonton, Almeley
Herefordshire HR3 6QH

First published by Logaston Press 2002
Reprinted 2003
Copyright © Derek Draisey 2002

ISBN 1 873827 13 X

Set in Times and Baskerville by Logaston Press
and printed in Great Britain by
Bell & Bain Ltd, Glasgow

Contents

Acknowledgements

To Ann with grateful thanks for all her love and patience, for all the help with this work, and to her daughter, Sarah, for her word-processing. Special thanks also to the staff at the Swansea Reference Library for their willing assistance, which was at times astonishing, and to Mrs. B. Cardy and Mr. M. Gibbs at the Swansea Museum for their help in obtaining illustrations and providing information as to the where-abouts of items held elsewhere. Special thanks are also due to Mr. Joyner and other members of staff at the National Library of Wales, Aberystwyth, and to the staff at the County Archives, Swansea. The courteous assistance of all the above, and those noted below as regards specific illustrations, is commendable.

Many of the photographs and maps in the book are my own, but I would also like to specifically thank the following individuals and organizations for providing and giving permission to publish illustrations as follows: The Royal Commission on the Ancient and Historical Monuments of Wales for the plan of the Roman Fort at Loughor on p.3; Logaston Press for the photograph on p.48; CADW; Welsh Historic Monuments, Crown Copyright for the plans of Swansea Castle on p.80; the Vicar of Swansea for the drawing of the Hugh Johnys brass on p.88; the *Evening Post* for the photograph of the model of the Plas on p.91; the University of Wales, Bangor, for the print of Matthew Cradock's tomb on p.93; the British Library for the illustration of Rowland Laugharne on p.105; the National Museum and Galleries of Wales, Cathays Park, Cardiff for the painting of Col. Philip Jones on p.106 and Francis Place's drawing on p.117; the National Library of Wales, Aberystwyth for the Cromwellian Market by John Nixon on p.130; the County Archives, County Hall, Swansea for the Tithe Map of 1845 on p.20, the Bucks' view on p.125, and the post-card depicting Swansea's markets over time on p.144; and to the City & County of Swansea: Swansea Museum Collection for the following: Iron Age bowl on p.2, Swansea Castle plan on p.55, drawing of Major-General Rowland Dawkin on p.107, the Townhall of 1820 on p.112, engravings by Thomas Rothwell on pp.124, 125 and 128, Paul Padley's view of Swansea on p.131, the Mumbles Railway by J. Ashford on p.142 and the drawing of the Town Hall on p.145.

CHAPTER I
Before the Norman Conquest

According to the Roman historian, Tacitus, the people who occupied south-east Wales in the late first century A.D. were the Silures, whom he described as swarthy with curly-hair. Their appearance and the fact that, in his mind, South Wales lay opposite Spain led him to believe that Spain was their country of origin. Archaeological evidence does not support such a hypothesis. Tacitus has nothing to say about the extent of Silurian territory, but it is thought that they occupied what is now south-east Wales and the adjoining English counties; Gower may have been their most westerly locality.

The Romans had invaded southern Britain in 43 A.D. Four years later the first Roman governor, Plautius, was succeeded by Ostorius Scapula, an event marked by an attack by tribes outside the Roman province. Scapula's response was to stamp out the opposition using auxiliaries—non-Roman citizens from all parts of the empire. In the year 51 a detachment of legionaries engaged in building a fort in Silurian territory was suddenly attacked and suffered the loss of its prefect, eight centurions and other troops. Relief forces were sent, but a foraging party was put to flight. It took units from two legions along with a number of auxiliary cohorts to bring the situation under control—or so it seemed until two auxiliary cavalry cohorts marched into a trap; the auxiliaries who were taken prisoner were distributed as slaves throughout Wales.

Scapula vowed to exterminate the Silures, but he died the following year. By the time his successor, Didius Gallus, arrived on the scene a legion had suffered defeat and the Silures were running amok over a wide area. The details of his and subsequent campaigns are obscure and remain so for the next 22 years. It is left to the archaeologist to make sense of the vague statements made by Tacitus, and the evidence, such as it is, suggests that by the late 50s the main legionary base was at Usk, a fortress supported by an unknown number of auxiliary forts, whilst Clyro and Cardiff may have been garrisoned by detachments of legionaries. Then, with the arrival of Britain's tenth governor, Julius Frontinus, in late 73 or early 74, the fog begins to clear a little, for Tacitus records that he 'defeated the Silures, overcoming their valour and the physical difficulties of their land'.

Worms Head, Rhosili (Worm is Old English for Dragon). In times past, superstitious seamen could easily have mistaken the island for a sea monster, especially when it loomed out of the mist

From the forts and roadways that were established as a result of his campaign, it seems likely that Frontinus chose to make several seaborne landings, and established marching camps on the high ground between the valleys. No such camps have been found in Gower, but on a ridgeway between the Swansea and Neath valleys the remains of a marching camp have been found at Coelbren, the banks enclosing an area of 35 acres, large enough to accommodate a legion and several auxiliary cohorts. The siting of this and other marching camps suggest that Frontinus executed a series of pincer movements from the coastal plains and from the Cardiff-Usk-Clyro line of legionary forts.

As part of a long-term strategy the whole of Silurian territory was studded with auxiliary forts linked by a network of roads, each fort separated from its nearest neighbour by a day's march, and all based on the new legionary fortress at Caerleon, the regimental headquarters of the Second Augusta Legion for the next 300 years. One auxiliary fort was sited at Neath (*Nidum*); another was situated at Loughor and, according to the 3rd century *Antonine Itinerary*, this fort was named *Leucarum*, from Leuc, the name of the river, meaning bright or shinning water.

The actual location of *Leucarum* did not come to light until 1969, when archaeologists discovered part of the fort wall and the foundations of an internal corner-turret in the side of the mound on which Loughor Castle stands. The turret proved

Early Iron-Age 'A' pottery found at Bacon Hole reassembled from the pieces found

to be the south-east corner of the fort which, shaped like a playing card, occupied the sloping ground between the castle and the Loughor estuary. It is believed that *Leucarum* occupied an area of approximately five acres, large enough to accommodate a mixed cohort of auxiliary infantry and cavalry (*cohors quingenaria equitata*) which, at full strength, would have numbered 608 men under the command of a prefect (*praefecti cohors*) who was a Roman citizen.

When the auxiliaries arrived at *Leucarum* in about the year 75 they constructed a fort which they surrounded with a ditch backed up by a huge earthen rampart. The rampart was contained by a massive, outward-facing palisade, perhaps 5m high, behind which the rampart sloped inwards over a distance of about 6m. Many years later, probably during the reign of Trajan (98 - 117), the palisade was replaced by a metre-thick stone wall. Then, about 130, the internal area was reduced by the construction of another wall which cut off the south-western half of the fort not long before the site was abandoned.

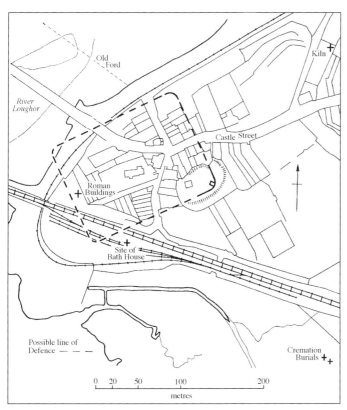

Loughor: area occupied by the Roman fort Leucarum, *showing the location of the south-eastern corner turret; also the 12th-century castle mound in which the turret was found in 1969. The 'old' ford could be used for a period of four hours during ebb tide*

Frontinus, having defeated the Silures, does not appear to have dealt harshly with them, although it is quite likely that many of their young men would have been drafted into the Roman army to become, perhaps, one of a dozen British auxiliary cohorts that are known to have served in the Army of the Danube. There is no evidence to support the idea that Silurian hill-forts were systematically destroyed. Roman pottery found in five Gower hill-forts is evidence that the locals continued to live in defended settlements even in the 2nd century. (A shard of mid-2nd century Samian ware was actually found under the ramparts of a hill-fort on Kilvey Hill, proving that the fort had been built long after the Roman conquest.)

In the space of a generation or more, *Venta Silurum* (Caerwent), the capital of the *Respublica Civitatus Silurum*, came into existence, where the leading men of the tribe became members of an *ordo* (a council) which managed the affairs of the *Civitas* (the tribal area) of the Silures. In the 2nd century villas begin to appear in the eastern parts of Silurian territory, a sign of a productive villa economy, one in which the great landowners could afford to own luxurious town houses. Further west, there seems to have been some sort of settlement in the Castle Street/Wind Street area of Swansea where fragments of a Roman period cooking pot and early 4th-century coins have been found, and a villa at Oystermouth where fragments of a mosaic pavement were found in the churchyard of All Saints Church along with shards of Roman pottery and coins.

The Roman administration of Britain came to an end about 410, leaving the country without an army and open to attack. Britain soon fragmented into numerous petty kingdoms, often warring among themselves; even the *Civitas* of the Silures did not survive as an entity. This chaotic state of affairs rendered the western seaboard of Britain open to Irish conquest and colonization, but all was not lost. The *Historia Brittonum*, written in the 9th century by the Celtic monk, Nennius, relates that some-time before or after 410 Cunedda, ruler of the Votadini, came from what is now Northumberland and expelled the Irish from North Wales with great slaughter; it is also stated by Nennius that he recovered Gower and the district of Kidwelly.

Whatever element of truth lies behind the story, there is plenty of evidence to support an Irish presence in Wales, particularly in the counties of Cardiganshire and Pembrokeshire where they established a royal dynasty—but what of Gower? Ogham was an alphabet of 23 characters used by the Irish, and is found as parallel chisel marks on the edges of stones. One Ogham inscription appears on the Roman altar found at *Leucarum*, a commemoration that is difficult to read. The Irish prefix *ach* appears in Clydach, a place-name that points to a stony river bed. Welsh *cnwch* as in Cnwch Coch, Llansamlet, is a borrowing from the Irish word *cnoc*. One inscription and two place-names, however, do not give the impression that Gower was overrun by Irish immigrants, yet indicates their presence.

With the withdrawal of the Romans Britain entered the Dark Ages, so called for the lack of surviving records of the history of the period. Overall rule of Britain gradually subsided into a multiplicity of local 'kings', sometimes uniting against a common threat. During the period the Saxons were invited into eastern England to help guard the coast, but in due course mounted a 'putsch' against their hosts, and so began the gradual Saxon conquest of what became England.

Gower has always enjoyed a more favourable climate than most parts of Wales, but at the beginning of the Dark Ages the climate throughout Europe was wors-ening, with an increase in rainfall, floods and great frosts. The uplands appear to have been exhausted by 600, and there is no evidence of a return to upland farming in Wales until the 11th century, by which time conditions had improved to some-thing similar to what they are today.

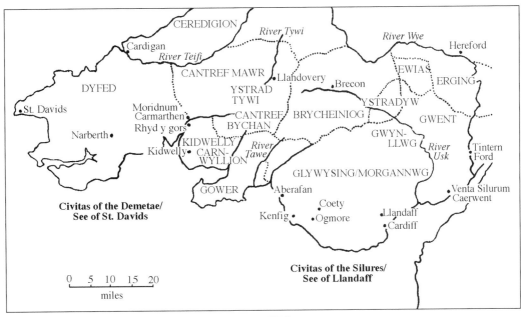

South Wales

Much of what is now moorland would have been adorned with oak and ash and silver birch to around 600 metres. In many places the valleys would have been impassable—dense oak woods on the flanks of rivers that sprawled across the landscape and reeds would have clogged the estuaries. Extensive bogs abounded.

The woods were the haunts of wild animals. A 12th-century charter states that the citizens of Swansea may have 'all the wild beasts which they can catch, except the stag, the hind, the wild boar and the marten'. Wolves were not uncommon—records state that, after the battle which took place on Garn Goch on 1 January 1136, 'the bodies of the fallen were horribly dragged about the fields and devoured by wolves', and if the traveller managed to avoid wolves there was always a chance, prior to the 7th century, of coming face to face with a brown bear.

Travellers approaching from the east would have made use of the old Roman road (of which nothing now remains) and crossed the Tawe about a mile inland from the estuary, using a Roman ford (at 6611 9468) which was discovered in the last century during excavation for a canal. The road undoubtedly continued westwards, but there is nothing to indicate its actual route until a remarkably straight stretch of modern roadway begins at the western end of Middle Road (at 6320 9599) to become the A4070 over Garn Goch Common to *Leucarum*. A traveller had then to ford the treacherous tidal waters of the Loughor estuary.

As the Roman road fell into disuse an alternative route from the ford at Neath may have passed near Llansamlet Church, crossed the Tawe above what is now Morriston and led to Llangyfelach, once the site of an important monastery; from there, via Penllergaer, the route continued to the Loughor estuary.

At some point in the Dark Ages, Gower—Gwyr in Welsh—became designated a commote, an administrative district comparable with an old English hundred. The earliest reference to its bounds is to be found in an appendage attached to a copy of a charter of King John, dated 23 February 1203, when he granted Gower to William de Breos III. It reads:

> The [River] Loughor separates Gower from [the neighbouring commote of] Carnwyllion. The [River] Aman and the [River] Llynfell, as far as Clawdd Owain, separates Gower from [the commotes of] Iscennen and Perfedd. The [River] Twrch separates Gower from the lordship of Brecknock. The [River] Tawe separates Gower from the lordship of Glamorgan as far as its confluence with the [River] Glais; from there the boundary follows the Glais as far as the Meinihirion [a standing stone on Mynydd Drumau] and from there it follows the Crymlyn [a stream which ran through Crymlyn Bog] as far as Pwllcynon [Cynon's Pool]; from there the boundary runs to the [River] Neath and from there to the sea.

Clearly the charter and the appendage is a title deed, though whether the territorial unit had the same boundary in the Dark Ages is impossible to say. Yet, undoubtedly the heart of Gower lay in the Peninsula and the majority of the population would have resided there. North of a line running from the Loughor and Tawe estuaries is hill country which, in turn, gives way to mountain ridges, often separated by steep-sided valleys, even ravines. It was here, in the northern hinterland, that the Celts held onto their language and way of life long after the Norman Conquest.

By the early 6th century Gower was definitely in the hands of a native dynasty, for several ecclesiastical sources relate that Glywys conquered much that had once been Silurian territory, Gower included, and that, on his death, when his kingdom was divided between his heirs, his son, Merchwyn, had Gower as his portion. Merchwyn appears in the *Liber Landavensis* (the Llandaff Charters) as a king who witnessed a grant of land in Gower to Dubricius, archbishop of Llandaff.

Merchwyn may have established himself in a position of strength. During work on the western end of the M4 Briton Ferry bridge (at the eastern extremity of the commote defined in the charter of 1203) the hill-fort of Hen Gastell was excavated and found to contain material dated to the 5th and 6th centuries. Fragments of pottery and glass point to trade links with Devon and Brittany, even the Mediterranean from whence came wine and oil. Merchwyn and his successors would have had other residences, one of which may have been at Old Henllys, Llandewi, where the faint remains of a hall, measuring 14.3m by 9m, are set within the north-east angle of a much larger enclosure, measuring 26m by 23m.

The 6th century is often regarded as the Age of the Saints, a period when ascetic followers of Christ established monastic settlements in which they could isolate themselves from the secular world. In all there are three sites in Gower that are known to have been monasteries or cells—Bishopston, Llangyfelach and the defunct hermitage on the island of Burry Holms.

The *Book of Llandaff* was written about 1130, but the writer claimed that part of the material had been copied from a much older book (no longer extant) called the *Llyfr Teilo*. What makes the *Book of Llandaff* invaluable is that it contains 149 charters which record the transfer of property, providing the names of those involved in the transactions and the witnesses present. Several of these charters refer to one Gwrgant the Great, a king who ruled Gower in the late 6th century, though why he should be dubbed 'Great' is unknown.

When Gwrgant died, Gower passed into the hands of a new dynasty, the founder of which, Tewdrig, ruled the plains of southern Gwent until, about 580, he became a hermit after commending his realm to his son, Meurig. Then, in 584, the kingdom was threatened by two Saxon warlords, Ceawlin and Cuthwain. Tewdrig was recalled to do battle and was slain at Tintern Ford, while his son, Meurig, pursued the defeated enemy, killing Cuthwain and forcing Ceawlin to retreat. Meurig then embarked on a policy of expansion, marrying Onbrawst, the daughter of Gwrgant the Great, and on the death of Gwrgant he inherited his father-in-law's kingdom.

Further charters indicate how Meurig's kingdom grew as his descendants acquired further property, until, by the early 8th century, there is but one kingdom in south-east Wales—Glywysing—which spread over the pre-1974 counties of Glamorgan, Monmouth and southern Herefordshire. At times Glywysing had a sole ruler; sometimes it was shared between brothers, even cousins, but unlike other parts of Wales it seems always to have remained as one kingdom.

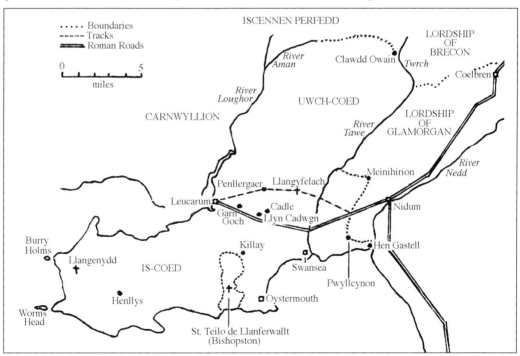

Dark Age sites and the bounds of Gower as they appear in King John's charter

Burry Holms, site of an early hermitage

Below the king were the *uchelwyr*, the free men who held land, most of it ancestral, often scattered far and wide, and with that land went the right to attend tribal meetings and the duty to enforce tribal law. Below the *uchelwyr* were the sons and grandsons, variously termed *noblis* in Latin, *bonheddig* in Welsh, 'men of stock' in English. These men were apparently settled on their father's (or grandfather's) land, but only after the death of their fathers (or grandfathers) did they become *uchelwyr*. When an *uchelwr* died, leaving two or more sons—regardless as to whether they were half-brothers, legitimate or not—his lands and moveable property were shared equally between them, a practice known as gavelkind. In cases where one son had died, then grandsons could lay claim to what would have been their father's share.

At the bottom of the social scale came slaves, an arrangement that continued well into the 13th century. The majority were slaves by birth, though in origin some of them may have been captives from cross-border raids as is suggested by the Saxon woman who, about 740, was given as part-payment for land. Free men could also be made slaves as a punishment for crimes such as theft. Slaves were accounted as chattels, to be bought and sold for the price, in later centuries, of four cows.

Our only indication as to what percentage of the population were slaves comes from the *Domesday* survey of 1086-7, which shows that in Cornwall—then a thoroughly Celtic region—21% of the population were slaves, and in the Welsh borderland 17% of the population were either slaves or oxmen. The percentage may have been higher in earlier centuries.

From the mid-10th century onwards, Owain ap Hywel Dda ruled the territory of the Demetae in south-west Wales—the kingdom of Deheubarth as it had become known—until advancing years forced him to hand over the reins to his son, Einion. In 970 and again in 977 Einion ravaged Gower, a preliminary, perhaps, to subjugating Glywysing which, by then, had been renamed Morgannwg—Morgan's Land. Einion may have gained control over Morgannwg, if only for a short time, for in 984 he was slain by the *uchelwyr* of Gwent—the eastern part of Morgannwg. Einion's brother, Maredudd, then succeeded to the kingdom of Deheubarth, but in 992 his position was challenged by Einion's son, Edwin.

In 992 Edwin ab Einion, aided by Edylfi the Saxon with a great host, ravaged all the territory of Maredudd in Deheubarth; that is, Ceredigion, Dyfed, Gower and Kidwelly and took hostages from the whole territory, which indicates that Gower had ceased to be part of Morgannwg. For the next hundred years or so it was linked politically with Kidwelly, Cantref Mawr and Cantref Bychan to form the territory of Ystrad Tywi.

Throughout the 11th century the kings of Deheubarth and Morgannwg fought each other frequently, with the result that Gower changed hands several times before finally reverting to the kingdom of Deheubarth in or soon after 1081. There are several place-names in Gower that point to the conflict: Cadle means 'place of battle', Penllergaer 'the head of the camp', and Cil-lle (Killay) 'place of retreat'. There is a also a tradition which states that 'the western tribes, defeated at Cadle after the death of their leader, who died of wounds whilst drinking at the well which still bears his name, fled in confusion towards the nearest ford of the River Loughor, and were routed a second time on the plains of Garn Goch [red stones] which took its name from the bloodshed which occurred there'. The well is that of Llyn Cadwgan, located near Llewitha Bridge, Fforestfach, and Cadwgan may be the king mentioned in the *Book of Llandaff* who reigned over Gower, Kidwelly and Cantref Bychan during the time of William the Conqueror (1066-87).

Another tradition states that Einion of Deheubarth was unhorsed in a bog that has perpetuated his name—Gorseinion. Is this the place where the *uchelwyr* of Gwent killed him? The Vikings, too, had a part to play in the conflict, although the only evidence of a Viking attack comes from the *Annales Cambriae* which records that, in 986, a host of Black Gentiles came to the Severn Sea and, landing in Gower, despoiled the possessions of the natives and burned the monastery of Llangenydd.

Rhys ap Tewdwr became king of Deheubarth in 1079, 13 years after William the Conqueror had seized the kingdom of England and installed his Norman followers along the March—the Welsh borderland—with power to take land from the Welsh and rule it in their own right. Rhys had a troublesome reign, several times having to fight off rival dynasties, and on one occasion had to flee to Ireland where he raised a fleet and returned to defeat his enemies. In the meantime, the Normans were nibbling away at the border kingdoms of Gwent, Brycheiniog and Powys.

There is a tradition that Rhys sent his son, Cynon, on an ill-fated raid into Morgannwg, on his return from which he was pursued so hard by his father's enemies that, on his approach to Gower, he tried to escape through Crymlyn Bog where he drowned along with many of his men; that place has borne the name Pwllcynon ever since.

In 1093 the situation worsened, for the Norman advance into Brycheiniog threatened Deheubarth. Rhys went on the offensive in support of Brycheiniog, but was slain near Brecon in April, leaving Deheubarth without a leader. In May the dynasty of Powys plundered Dyfed. In July the dam burst; Norman troops under the earl of Shrewsbury swept through the mountain passes of mid-Wales and overran Ceredigion and Dyfed, establishing castles at Cardigan, Pembroke and many other places. The lowlands of Morgannwg, too, may have been seized about this time. By the end of the year the greater part of Wales was in Norman hands.

During the early part of the following year William Rufus, king of England, was in Normandy when a revolt broke out in Gwynedd that quickly spread the length and breadth of Wales. At the close of the year almost all the castle in Ceredigion and Dyfed and been razed to the ground—but the Normans soon had their revenge. In 1095 they 'ravaged Gower, Kidwelly and Ystrad Tywi [meaning in this context Cantref Mawr and Cantref Bychan] so that they remained waste for many years'.

The following year the men of Brycheiniog, Gwent and Gwynllwg were in open revolt again, causing the Normans to move a host into Gwent, only to be defeated by the Welsh in a place called Celli Tarfawg. Thereupon the Normans raided Brycheiniog, intending to destroy the land completely, but having achieved nought, they were returning home when they were cut off at Aber-llech and totally routed. Then, led by Rufus, a great host marched into South Wales in 1097, but the Welsh avoided them, knowing that they would not dare enter the woods, and they watched their enemies hover about the plains until they returned home empty-handed.

Henry I had reigned for two years when, in 1102, Robert de Belleme, earl of Shrewsbury, and his brother, Arnulf, lord of Pembroke, were accused of plotting against him. Henry advanced slowly into Robert's territory and, with the intention of detaching the earl from his Welsh vassals, offered one Iorwerth of Powys a great deal of territory, including Gower, Kidwelly and Ystrad Tywi.

After the revolt had been put down, Henry went back on his promises and gave Gower, Kidwelly and Ystrad Tywi to Hywel ap Goronwy. In the same year Goronwy ap Rhys—who may have ruled the aforesaid territories after the death of his father, Rhys ap Tewdwr—was seized and died in prison. Henry's next move was to frustrate the new ruler, Hywel ap Goronwy, which he did in 1105 by ordering Richard fitzBaldwin to repair the ruined castle at Rhyd-y-gors, which is believed to have been sited about one mile south of Carmarthen, on the east bank of the Tywi. Ruined or not, Rhyd-y-gors stood within Hywel's territory, the keeping of which the king had entrusted to him, and Hywel sought to destroy the castle. Houses and crops were burnt, the land ravaged, some of the settlers slaughtered, but the castle remained undisturbed.

In 1106, Gwgan ap Meurig, who had nurtured Hywel's son, invited Hywel to his house, then sent word to fitzBaldwin. FitzBaldwin came at night and had his men surround the house, then raise a shout. Hywel called to his companions, but they had fled. When Hywel tried to escape he was caught, half strangled, then dragged to fitzBaldwin, who cut off his head and took it to the castle at Rhyd-y-gors. Gower, Cydweli and Ystrad Tywi was now leaderless, open to attack, as Deheubarth had been 13 years earlier—it was to seal Gower's fate.

CHAPTER II
Conquest and Settlement

The fact that reliable sources are silent as to how Gower became subject to Norman rule has proved reason for some to assume that, after Hywel ap Goronwy's death, the take-over was a relatively peaceful affair. The assumption is flawed for several reasons, one being that the scale of usurpation and colonization which took place in the peninsula could not have been achieved without a measure of force.

Land was a Welshman's most valuable asset, indeed, without land he had no standing. It is, therefore, unlikely that the native Welsh would have stood by while armed men laid claim to their lands. They were a people who, in the late 12th century, were described by Gerald, archdeacon of Brecon, in his *Description of Wales* 'as raised to the use of arms, for not only their nobles, but all the people are trained for war'. Even Henry II (1154-89), paid homage to their tenacity when he wrote, in a letter to the emperor of Constantinople: 'in a certain part of this island there are a people called Welsh, so bold and ferocious that though unarmed they do not fear to encounter an armed body of men, being ready to shed their blood for their country, to sacrifice their lives for renown'.

That they were to be feared is borne out by the account of a Breton who observed them in Northern France in 1196:

> They resort to the woods and are skilful in marching through difficult ways, not hampered by footwear or armour; they are taught to endure cold, never to give up toil. They carry a sole weapon: a pike, battle-axe, bow, lance, a few hunting spears or javelins. They rejoice in plunder and bloodshed, and it is rare that any of them die, except through wounds. If anyone throws it upon them that one of their kinsmen died without killing someone, they consider it a dishonour. They eat cheese and half-cooked flesh, the blood of which they squeeze out by pressing the meat in the cleft of a tree. They slaughter pitilessly, young and old, parents and children.

But did this apply to all Welshmen? Or just a certain class? There is a discrepancy in what Gerald had to say in that not all Welshmen were proficient in the use of arms, for fighting was the privilege of free men. The unfree, the peasants and slaves, were not called upon to fight, at least, not in the 12th century. While there can be no doubt that free men were the dominant element in Welsh society, they were not necessarily the most numerous class. The *Domesday* survey of 1086-7, which records the ownership of land in England in the Welsh borderland, shows that in the former county of Flintshire only 31% of the population were classified as free.

Prior to its conquest, Gower had been one of perhaps 13 commotes in the lordship of Hywel ap Goronwy, and as such may have had its own territorial lord. In his *Morganiae Archaiographia* written some 460 years after the event, Rice Merrick claims that Rhydderch the Great had been the last Welsh lord of Gower before it was conquered by the Normans, though this is questionable. Whoever he was, he would have had his a llys—a winter court—possibly at Trewyddfa, an important manor when first mentioned in documents relating to Norman times—and a summer camp, this possibly at Penllergaer, its proximity close to what became known in post-conquest times as the *Portmead*—'the Lord's Meadow'; he also had one or more hunting lodges.

His most important officer was the *Penteulu*—'head of household'—usually a close relative whose primary role was to command his lord's bodyguard which consisted of the lightly-armed sons of free men who, at the age of 14, were commended to serve their lord for seven years.

Henry de Newburgh I, earl of Warwick, also known as Harry Beaumont—Beaumont being his father's name—was the first Norman lord of Gower. Long after his death he was described as studious and of retiring disposition; that said, he was still a man to be reckoned with: the king's foster-brother and a member of the king's inner circle of counsellors.

It seems likely that, following the murder of Hywel ap Goronwy, Harry Beaumont was granted right of conquest, a mandate to ensure that no one else marched on Gower. For someone with a peaceful disposition this was a godsent opportunity to make himself out to be a conqueror without any real danger to himself. His huge estates in England and Normandy furnished him with sufficient men through feudal service, the backbone of whom were heavily-armed horsemen—not knights in the accepted sense, but rough and ready men-at-arms—with a ratio of one man-at-arms for every ten foot soldiers, many of them archers. By and large the foot soldiers were Saxons.

Beaumont's army could have arrived in Gower by land or sea. As to when this happened, it may be assumed that it was sometime between the death of Hywel ap Goronwy in 1106 and a Welsh attack, in 1116, on a castle at Swansea which belonged to Beaumont, possibly during the summer of 1107, for in March that year, Robert fitzHamon, lord of Glamorgan died as a result of a severe head wound and, lacking an heir, his lordship had escheated to the king; thus the king was in a position to place the Marcher lords of Glamorgan at the disposal of Beaumont, this would have been necessary as only the Marcher lords were accustomed to combating the guerilla warfare of the Welsh.

In writing about the Marcher lords of his day the historian, Orderic Vitalis, described them as extremely arrogant and wilful men, ruled by their greed and a desire to lord it over others, sadistic warriors, addicted to pleasure, their hunting forays wreaking havoc in fields and woods. Two such barons were probably involved in the campaign from the start, William de Londres and Payn de Turberville—Payn and his descendants and the descendants of de Londres appear in a variety of documents relating to Gower throughout the 12th century; both men were also active participants in Robert fitzHamon's seizure of the fertile Vale of Glamorgan.

William de Londres had been entrusted with the keeping of Ogmore Castle, the most westerly outpost of the conquerors of Glamorgan at that time, but Payn de Turberville is the more interesting character. He may have been a Breton; if so, it is likely that he could converse in Welsh. According to a tradition, Payn had been given men and marched into the foothills of Glamorgan to be met by Morgan ap Meurig, the Welsh lord of Coety. Morgan, knowing himself to be outmatched, suggested to Payn that, instead of doing battle, he should marry his daughter, Sybil, or fight him in single combat. Payn settled for the easier option and married Sybil, thereby inheriting his father-in-law's commote.

The objective of the campaign would be twofold: construct a castle that could be supplied and reinforced by sea, then terrorize the natives into submission—it rarely failed. The site chosen for the castle was at Abertawe (the Welsh name for Swansea), meaning 'mouth of the Tawe River'.

At Swansea, in 1913, excavation for town improvements between Worcester Place and Castle Street revealed the existence of an early castle, probably a motte and bailey, built on a knoll that was surrounded on three sides by two watercourses and, on the east, by a steep slope to the estuary. The northern watercourse, from a point about 30 metres south of Welcome Lane, ran to the Strand. On the west a second watercourse ran about midway between Worcester Place and Castle Street, then turned eastwards down Castle Lane to the Strand. The watercourses on both the north and west are

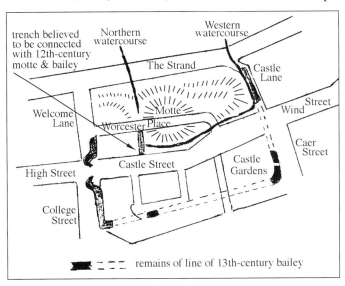

Swansea's 12th-century motte is believed to have straddled what is now Worcester Place. It was surrounded on three sides by watercourses (which were converted into ditches) and on the east by a steep slope to the Strand

assumed to have been made into ditches, the spoil dumped on the knoll to heighten its elevation, giving it the appearance of a pudding-shaped mound, the motte, on the summit of which a wooden tower would have been erected. A bailey, squarish in plan, occupied the fairly level area of what is now Castle Street and housed several buildings, the largest and most important of which was the hall. Apart from a ditch, the bailey was protected by a palisade. One or more draw-bridges, protected perhaps by wooden towers, spanned the bailey ditch. Further west, beyond the bailey, the ground fell away; the slope can be seen in the walkway between Castle Gardens and David Evans' Store.

The bailey was separated from the motte by a ditch (originally the western watercourse) and a walkway, supported by piles, extended from the bailey, across the ditch, and up the slope of the motte to where a gate barred entry to the tower. No ditch was necessary on the eastern side of the motte as a steep slope fell to the Strand. It should be noted that the River Tawe, diverted in the 19th century to accommodate the docks, originally flowed close to the Strand—'the Margin of the Sea'—enabling ships to get close to the castle.

A little to the south, in the area occupied by the 14th-century castle that can be seen today, there was once a graveyard, probably connected with the motte and bailey mentioned above.

The records provide no clues as to how the Welsh responded when the Normans set to work building a castle—as to whether they made sporadic attacks or, as at Rhyd-y-gors, they left the castle and the garrison undisturbed. They may even have sued for peace at an early stage, in which case it would have been safe for Harry Beaumont to come to Gower to accept formal submissions, to dictate terms and lay claim to certain lands. The northern hinterland was of little use to him, a wasteland unsuitable for manorial cultivation, whereas the fertile lowland was the prize with which he rewarded his followers. So Gower was henceforth to be of two parts: *Wallicana* (the Gower of Welshmen) and *Anglicana* (the Gower of Normans and Saxons), which later became known as the English county of Gower. Within the Englishry certain estates, such as Trewyddfa and Pennard, were set aside as demesne manors, the personal property of Harry and his successors.

As a reward for their services many of the earl's leading men, the men-at-arms in particular, were given confiscated land, manorial estates that have been variously termed mense lordships, fiefs and fees, which they held by military tenure on the understanding that, each year, they performed 40 days castle guard at Abertawe, although it is not known whether this requirement would have applied to the Marcher lords.

A charter of 1306 lists 13 'old knights' fiefs' as Penrice, Port Eynon, Oxwich, Henllys, Weobley, Scurlage Castle, Reynoldston, Knelston, Penmaen, Nicholaston, Furzehill, Fernhill and Pilton, and Stembridge. Unfortunately the list is suspect in that its originator, William de Breos VII, may have doctored it to suit his own ends; that said, five of these fiefs—Penrice, Port Eynon, Oxwich, Nicholaston and

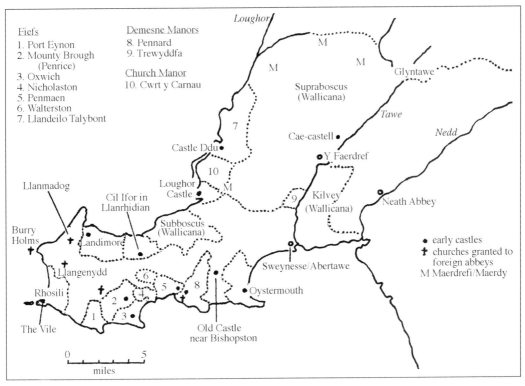

Fiefs
1. Port Eynon
2. Mounty Brough (Penrice)
3. Oxwich
4. Nicholaston
5. Penmaen
6. Walterston
7. Llandeilo Talybont

Demesne Manors
8. Pennard
9. Trewyddfa

Church Manor
10. Cwrt y Carnau

Loughor

M

M

M

Glyntawe

Supraboscus (Wallicana)

Tawe

Nedd

Castle Ddu •

Cae-castell •

7

• Y Faerdref

10

Llanmadog

Loughor Castle •

M

Cil Ifor in Llanrhidian

9

Kilvey (Wallicana)

Neath Abbey

Burry Holms ✝

Landimore

Subboscus (Wallicana)

• early castles
✝ churches granted to foreign abbeys
M Maerdrefi/Maerdy

Llangenydd ✝

6

Sweynesse/Abertawe

Rhosili

2

5

8

4

• Oystermouth

The Vile

1

3

Old Castle near Bishopston

0   5

miles

Gower in the 12th century

Penmaen—plus the lord's manor of Pennard, stand apart from the others in that later documentary evidence suggests that they were colonized by people from the south-west of England. Surveys carried out in the 16th to 18th centuries show that the measurement of land within the five fiefs and the manor of Pennard was based on a 9 foot pole, a measurement widely used on the opposite side of the Bristol Channel. It is likely that these estates, all of them in the vicinity of Oxwich Bay, were among the first to be created. The incoming settlers were called customary tenants, or *coloni*, and worked the manorial estates of their masters, the holders of fiefs.

Elsewhere in the peninsula, colonization appears to have been less intense, but enough for Isaac Hamon to comment in the late 16th century that 'in former times all the people of the Gower Peninsula, both high and low did speak the Old English; on the *south side* they did pronounce their words something like the west of England; on the *north side* they inclined more to the Welsh, and mixed some Welsh words amongst their Old English'. This Old English which Hamon referred to had its origin in the former counties of Devon and Somerset and, in later times, the dialect was reinforced by cross-Channel trade between Gower and the two counties.

To protect themselves and their *coloni* the holders of fiefs built a series of small castles, of which 10 can be identified, though there may be others either lost in the

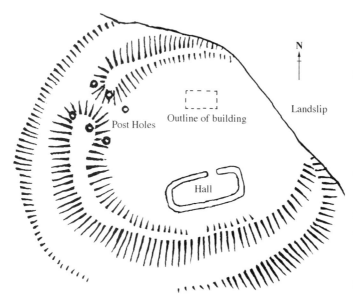

Castle Tower ring-work, Penmaen, home of the Hareng family, was burnt on at least two occasions and finally abandoned in the early 13th century

landscape, or wrongly classified as Iron Age hill-forts. Two castles were sited at fords on the River Loughor to safeguard against incursions from the west, one at Loughor itself, the other near Pontardulais. Four castles—one on North Hill Tor, another on Cil Ifor, a third near Bishopston, a fourth at Oystermouth—are arrayed in an arc across the peninsula to guard the Englishry against attacks from the north and from across the Loughor estuary; their siting resembles the Lansker borderland of southern Pembroke, where a series of castles guarded 'little England beyond Wales'. The remaining four are located in the vicinity of Oxwich Bay—Mounty Brough near Penrice Church, Norton Camp to the west of Oxwich village, Penmaen and Pennard.

Loughor Castle. The summit of the mound was encircled, first by a palisade and later by a stone wall. A succession of gate-towers have stood on the west, some in wood, some in stone like the late 13th- to early 14th-century remains seen today

Only one of these castles is of motte and bailey type; known as Castle Du, it stands near Pontardulais. The motte, which 80 years ago stood to a height of 9m, can be seen by road-users travelling westwards on the M4 as they approach the Pontardulais turn-off—it has the appearance of a pudding-shaped mound to the left of the motorway.

Eight of these castles fall into the category of ring-works, the best example being Castle Tower, Penmaen. Located on a promontory overlooking Three Cliffs Bay, Castle Tower consists of a semi-circular, rock-cut ditch, the spoil used to form an inner bank which, on the east, is absent due to landslide; this bank would have been surmounted by a palisade of pointed stakes, or a box-like timber frame which enabled the defenders to patrol the ramparts and ward off Welsh attacks. Excavations in 1960-61 revealed that six large posts had provided the framework for a 6m square timber gatehouse, the first floor serving as living quarters for the lord in times of peace. When threatened with attack, narrow windows in this first-floor hall would have served as ports through which arrows or bolts could be directed at the attackers. Gate-houses such as this may have been common to all Gower ring-works; they were, however, vulnerable to fire and the Penmaen gate-house showed signs of having been destroyed in a conflagration, after which it appears to have been replaced by a narrow gateway. Two buildings of different dates, one of them undoubtedly a hall, had stood within the ring-bank. Pottery finds suggest that the site had been abandoned before the mid-13th century.

Oystermouth stands alone in that there is no trace of an earth and timber castle there, although the chronicles imply that a castle at Oystermouth was attacked and burnt in 1116, and the chronicles are explicit that in 1215 Oystermouth Castle was stormed and burnt by Rhys Ieuanc and his men.

The motte of Castle Du, Pontardulais. In 1215 the castle was attacked by Rhys Ieunac and the garrison put to fire and sword

The remains of halls have been found at two ring-work castles—Pennard and Penmaen—and a third has been unearthed in the besanded village of Rhosili (on the warren below and on the seaward side of Rhosili Down). The remains of all three halls consisted of low, dry-stone walls, rectangular in plan, with rounded corners. The one discovered inside Pennard Castle proved to be 18m long, divided into a private chamber, the 'hall' itself where everyone dined and the lord attended to business, and two small service rooms. Each of these buildings was once covered by a huge ridge roof made of thatch or shingle. A hall of this type probably occupied the bailey at Abertawe.

The chronicles provide the bare outlines of the history of the period, whereas charters provide details such as the ownership of land, and the names of people who witnessed the transactions. Well-to-do landowners may appear to have been generous benefactors to religious institutions, but it should be remembered that these men were often unscrupulous, yet aware that their actions might lead to eternal damnation. When they made a donation they expected something in return which, all too often, took the form of monks praying for their souls and the souls of those dear to them.

It was important that the boundaries of gifted land were set out in a charter, so that they could be referred to whenever there was a dispute. As time went by it was considered necessary to have the original grants confirmed by kings or bishops, and monasteries and other ecclesiastical institutions were quite willing to pay bishops and kings for the service. In the case of Gower the original charters have been lost, but the donations are known through confirmation grants made by bishops in particular. Without these confirmation grants our knowledge of 12th-century Gower would be sparse to say the least.

One of the earliest references to a holder of a fief comes from a confirmation of Peter de Leia, bishop of St. Davids (1176-98): 'in the land which Geoffrey Panchefot held the fief of Llandeilo Talybont, which is between the waters of the Lliw and Loughor and between the streams which fall into the Loughor, which Henry de Vilers [Villiers in some documents] gave to the monks [of Neath Abbey] in alms, with the consent of Henry de Warwick; the Chapel of St. Michael, with the land and pasture and other easements, which they have of Henry de Vilers'.

This charter was subsequently confirmed by King John (1199-1216). It is clear from this and other charters that Henry de Vilers had held the two fiefs of Loughor and Talybont, and that he had subenfoeffed a Geoffrey Panchefot at Talybont. Neath Abbey had been founded in 1130, and the Henry de Warwick who gave his consent was a younger son of Harry Beaumont, who does not appear to have taken over the administration of Gower until about 1138, indicating that the original grant must have taken place after c.1138. The land which Henry de Vilers gave in alms became the Grange of Cwrt y Carnau.

What happened to the de Vilers family after Henry's death is difficult to ascertain. A Sir John de Viles witnessed a charter in 1320, but there is no indication as to what were his fiefs at that time. He certainly did not hold either Loughor or Llandeilo Talybont as both fiefs are recorded in a charter of 1306 as demesne manors of the lords of Gower.

A better known name is that of de Penres (Penrice). Initially the family held the castle and fief of Mounty Brough (known later as the fiefs of Penrice and Horton) and the fief of East Pilton (between Rhosili and Port Eynon). In a charter drawn up during the time of Bishop David (1147-76) a Robert de Penres is said to have granted the Church of St. Andrews (in the parish of Penrice) to the Order of Knights Hospitallers. The grant was confirmed by a John de Penres about 1180, and confirmed again by another Robert de Penres about 1200. In time the family became the most opulent in Gower, but died out in the early 15th century.

The *Liber Rubeus*, a document which lists the men-at-arms who held fiefs of William, earl of Warwick, in Gower in 1166, names Terricus Hareng as the holder of a fief; he is probably the ancestor of the Hareng expelled from Penmaen by Rhys Gryg in 1217, whose son, Philip, recovered the patrimony in 1241 on the instructions of King Henry III. An Adam Hering held the fief in 1320.

A William de Barry gave 30 acres from his fief of Walterston to Neath Abbey. This donation appears in a confirmation made by Peter de Leia. This must surely be a late 12th-century transfer because William de Barry made a point of notifying Bishop Gervase (1215-30) of his 30-acre gift. At a later date, following the surrender of Gower to Welsh forces in 1217, William de Barry wisely exchanged his fief of Walterston for 100 acres in Somerset which belonged to Neath Abbey, at which point Walterston ceased to be a fief, becoming a grange of the Abbey.

William de Londres may have been enfeoffed with Oystermouth and West Pilton, and probably other holdings. In 1141 his son, Maurice, made a gift of the income of Oystermouth Church to St. Peter's Abbey at Gloucester. The family expired in the male line in the early 13th century and, in a charter of 1306, Oystermouth is not listed as a fief, but as a demesne manor of the lords of Gower.

Payn de Turberville may have been the holder of what was once the extensive manor of Landimore, stretching from Rhosili to within a few miles of Crofty, an area with a predominantly Welsh population. In 1131 he caused a stir in ecclesiastical circles when his steward, Rabel, took the manor of Bishopton, the personal property of the bishop of Llandaff, which resulted in the pope advising the bishop to seek redress from the king.

The manor of Landimore, however, was gradually broken up, the result of land grants to religious houses, so that by the late 12th century it retained only the dispersed sub-manors of Rhosili, Landimore (the parish of Cheriton and possibly what later became the fief of Weobley) and Llanrhidian. A William de Turberville appears as the holder of the dispersed fief of Landimore in Earl William's returns of the late 12th century and, in a confirmation made by Peter de Leia, he is cited as the man who gave the churches of Rhosili, Landimore and Llanrhidian (with its chapel at Walterston) to the Order of Knights Hospitallers.

Significant changes were to take place on the south side of the peninsula, the dispersed habitat of the native Welsh being replaced by knights' fiefs. Each fief was a fairly compact community, the focal points of which where the residence of the local lord (often a descendant of a man-at-arms who took part in the conquest) and the local church. The majority of the settlers, the villagers, often referred to as customary tenants, *coloni* or villeins, were obliged to work their lord's demesne in return for a share in land that was common to the community. Much that had been wasteland was cleared to create an array of open fields, about half belonging to the local lord, the rest held by the villagers. Traces of an open field system can be found in the parish of Rhosili, south of the present-day church, where a bewildering array of fields known collectively as the Vile, or Great Field, were shared by the villagers of earlier times. Within the Vile each villager held a varying number of strip fields, long and narrow in shape and bounded by low, grass covered banks (commonly known as baulks) which served as raised paths. Today the Vile is enclosed by a dry-stone wall; many of the fields have lost their original strip shape and are now bounded by quite high banks. Small by today's standards, sheep became increasingly important, providing milk, fertilizer, meat and wool. Large flocks were subsequently kept by both landowners and by Neath Abbey to meet the growing demands of the wool merchants.

The division of Gower into Englishry and Welshry may echo the pre-conquest commotes of Is-coed and Uwch-coed, meaning lower and upper part of the woods respectively. Evidence for this comes from a legal document which records how William de Breos VII recovered possession of the 'two commotes of Is-coed and Uwch-coed which contain the whole of Gower'.

Almost everything that is known about 12th-century Gower relates to *Anglicana*, a multi-racial territory as the charter of 1306 is addressed to all men, both 'Welsh and English, within the English County of Gower'. Within *Wallicana* the people were for centuries exclusively Welsh, though whether they had their own Welsh lord is not known, for the

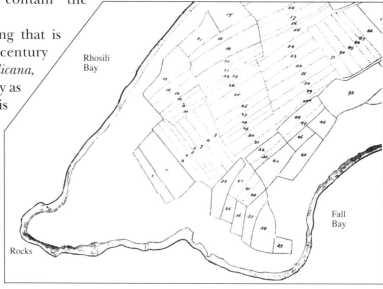

Part of The Vile near Worm's Head, showing the strip field system still preserved on an 1845 Tithe Map

The Taeogion

Much has been written about Welsh lords and land-holding free tribesmen, but in Welsh society there was a class less privileged than free men, though not slaves in the accepted sense. In England the people within this class were referred to as serfs and villeins, whereas in South Wales they were called *taeogion*. These bondsmen were invariably servile by birth. Yet birth alone did not account for their lowly status, but that they were tied to the land on which they lived and worked, and which they could not leave without the landowner's permission. Prior to the conquest, and perhaps after it, Welsh lords depended, in part, on the food renders of free tribesmen, but more so on the obligations of their *taeogion*.

Everything that was theirs: life, honour, property—all had a lower worth than that of a free man. It was possible for some of them to attain the status of a free man, providing that, with the lord's consent, they took up a profession such as that of a smith, bard or cleric, but the enfranchisement did not extend to a son unless he too took up the profession. Only the Church made any real attempt to set these people free, and this they did—with the agreement of the lord—by consecrating a church within a taeog community.

There were various types of bond communities; only the *maerdrefi* have left their mark on the landscape.

Sited on fertile ground near a river or stream, a *maerdref* was a demesne manor incorporating a small community of bondsmen, the ideal consisting of nine houses according to surviving law texts. A *maerdref*, often known as *Maerdy*, took its name from the officer, the *maer*, who was responsible for telling the *taeogion* what to grow and where. Part of the estate was the lord's table land, and part of it was held in common by the *taeogion*, the strips allocated to each *taeog* by the *maer*. On the outskirts of the estate were paid labourers—cottars in English—who were excluded from the common rights of the *maerdref* community, holding nothing more than vegetable plots. There is evidence to suggest that the following locations in Gower were once *maerdrefi*:

Maerdy, the name of a small community about a mile south of Ammanford

Rhyd-y-maedy, Gorseinon, the name preserved in the Mardy public house

Maerdy, near Blaen-nant-hir (725115)

Neuaddwen, near Garnant, where evidence of customary tenure can be found in 17th century surveys

Y Faerdref, Clydach—the name preserved in the Vardre public house—where a corn-mill and a fulling mill is mentioned in a 14th-century account. The demesne here may have been of some importance as the Cae-castell earthwork is only two miles to the north

Trewyddfa, in the Swansea valley, may have been a pre-conquest demesne which Harry Beaumont took for his own

The Mardy Hotel, site of a Welsh meardref *(maerdy) where bondsmen known as* taeogion *lived and worked the surrounding land*

There must have been scores of *maerdrefi* in the peninsula, none of which have left any trace, all of them the property of Welsh lords, but the *uchelwyr* also had their bondsmen, though the records for South Wales are silent about them. What is certain is that, at the time of the conquest, the *taeogion* were the most numerous class. The *Domesday* survey of 1086-7 records that, in north-east Wales about 52% of the Welsh population were *taeogion*. In earlier times the percentage is likely to have been much higher.

With the expiry of Welsh lords the distinction between freemen and taeogion gradually became blurred, and the number of *maerdrefi* declined until, by the 14th century, they had all but disappeared, the taeogion having become tenant farmers.

records are much more sparse. Rice Merrick refers to a Cadifor marrying Malt, the daughter and heiress of Llywelyn Ychan, Lord of Glyntawe 'and part of Gower', thereby becoming possessed of those parts. Unfortunately, the above statements cannot be verified, which leaves no Welsh aristocracy to refer to. There is a further problem in that *Wallicana* was itself sub-divided into two parts: *Supraboscus* and *Subboscus*, the Latin equivalents of upper and lower part of the woods respectively.

Subboscus was by far the smaller sub-division, incorporating what is now Crofty, Penclawdd and Three Crosses. If Gower had been two commotes in pre-conquest times, then little of the southern commote (Is-coed) survived under Norman rule. It is not know if *Subboscus* had its own lord, or whether it was linked politically with *Supraboscus* to the north. Obviously the Norman had no wish to absorb it—even today this part of Gower contrasts with the south coast and, in the

12th century, it can be confidently assume that *Subboscus*, as its name suggests, was a place full of woods.

Supraboscus was a mountainous hinterland, lying roughly to the north of the M4 motorway, an economic wilderness of woods and marshes, the soil suitable for little more than cultivating oats and rearing cattle. Within this wilderness lies the Cae-castell earthwork, about two miles north of Clydach, (694 047), believed to be a Welsh attempt at constructing a motte and bailey castle. It consists of a squarish enclosure on the edge of a ravine which protects it on its north-eastern side. The western half of the enclosure is dominated by a ridge of high ground which may have served the function of a motte. The choice of such a remote place for a castle, not far from the ridgeway over Mynydd Carnllechart, is testimony to the possible existence of a Welsh lord, one who could be confident that he would not be taken in a surprise attack from Abertawe. The earliest reliable reference to a local lord comes in 1287, when certain landowners of *Supraboscus* rebelled against the Norman lord, William de Breos VI. One of the rebels, Gruffudd Frych, held the title of lord of Glyntawe, a minor lordship within the neighbouring lordship of Brycheiniog. There is reason to believe that, apart from Glyntawe, Gruffudd Frych also held land in the north-eastern corner of *Supraboscus*, but it must be said that he does not appear to have been a resident of Gower.

Further south the evidence is just as wanting, for in 1348, when John de Mowbray confirmed to his tenants of *Subboscus* all their laws and customs, he made no reference to a Welsh lord. By the time of the earliest surviving financial records—which date from 1367 onwards—the landowners throughout Wallicana were paying their dues to the beadles of the Norman lord, William de Breos VII. It may be, that once the Welsh lords had expired, the landowners of Wallicana paid their dues to the Norman lords of Gower who, for the sake of peace, allowed them to live according to their ancient customs and laws.

Situated on the east bank of the River Tawe, the lordship of Kilvey causes historians to pause for thought. It is not known whether Kilvey had been part of Gower in pre-conquest times, or whether it became an appendage as a result of the foundation of Neath Abbey in 1130. It was certainly a part of Gower during the time of Henry de Newburgh II (*c.*1138 - post 1166) as he is known to have granted fishery rights in the area to Neath Abbey. In 1217 it became a Welsh fief, the result of Llywelyn ap Iorwerth, king of Gwynedd, granting it to Morgan Gam, lord of Afan. It remained the property of Morgan Gam's descendants until the mid-14th century, although their claim to Kilvey was often challenged by the Norman lords of Gower who considered it to be part of *Wallicana*. For the most part, Kilvey was thoroughly Welsh, and in the receiver's accounts of the early 14th century the landowners of Kilvey were still paying *Gwestfa* as their main rent—*Gwestfa* being the age-old food renders paid by free landowners to Welsh lords. Prior to Kilvey becoming a Welsh fief, an English community had taken root on the east bank of the Tawe, for Gerald tells us that, in 1188, whilst travelling to Abertawe, he stopped briefly at the church of St. Thomas, a Norman dedication in an area that later became part of the parish of Swansea.

Before returning to Warwick, Harry Beaumont had to appoint a seneschal—a steward—to administer his Marcher lordship, which comprised of both *Anglicana* and *Wallicana*. The earliest reference to this office comes from the *Pipe Rolls*; they establish William de Londres II—the grandson of William de Londres I—as seneschal in 1187, 1188 and 1192; he also appears as a witness to several charters relating to Gower. William de Londres I may have been Harry Beaumont's choice, he was, after all, lord of Ogmore, a Marcher baron with experience in managing a multi-racial lordship. However, he may have been committed to conquering the neighbouring commotes of Kidwelly and Carnwyllion on behalf of Roger, bishop of Salisbury, the king's chief advisor. His son, Maurice, certainly held Kidwelly Castle in 1136 on behalf of Bishop Roger, and his name also appears in documents relating to Gower. Another candidate with similar experience was Payn de Turberville, lord of Coety.

A seneschal was responsible for administering justice and for the security of the lordship. Apart from the men-at-arms who held fiefs and were obliged to do castle guard at Abertawe, the castle also had a standing garrison as a charter of William, lord of Gower (post 1166- 84), to the citizens of Swansea states: 'wherever my men-at-arms shall take grass for my horses, my burgesses similarly may take with them'. There is no mention of archers, but they would have constituted an important element in the garrison. Gerald states that Cardiff Castle was guarded by 120 men-at-arms, a figure that presumably includes retainers, and a numerous body of archers (usually three times the strength of mounted men), and a strong watch (provided by the townspeople no doubt). This may have amounted to a garrison of 500 men, plus the townspeople. The garrison at Abertawe may not have been so numerous, its size varying according to how serious a threat were the princes of West Wales, but it would still have been of sufficient strength to keep the Welsh of Gower in check.

It may seem surprising that castles such as Cardiff and Abertawe/Sweynesse had large garrisons. Yet both were administrative centres for their respective lordships, and the Roman army, which was far more efficient than any medieval host, saw fit to construct forts in Wales which were garrisoned by cohorts of between 500 and 1000 men; the Roman forts at Loughor (*Leucarum*) and Neath both had garrisons of at least 500 men.

A statement made by Gerald supports the view that Abertawe had a large garrison. In 1136 a battle was fought on the plains of Garn Goch, involving a large number of English troops—516 according to one account—and Gerald states that the Welsh 'defeated the English of those parts, many of them foot soldiers'. It is likely that many of the English troops came from fiefs in the peninsula, and that many were garrison troops from Abertawe. It was only when castles were rebuilt in stone that garrisons were reduced to much smaller numbers.

Rhys ap Tewdwr, the last native ruler of Deheubarth, had been slain by the Normans in 1093, and amid the chaos caused by invasion one of Rhys's sons, Gruffudd, a mere infant at the time, had been taken by kinsmen to Ireland to escape capture by his father's enemies. Twenty years later, Gruffudd returned to his homeland and for two years wandered peaceably, sometimes staying with Gerald de Windsor, his brother-in-law, sometimes with his own kin. In 1115 he rose in rebellion when, gathering a band of young hopefuls at his side, he attacked the foreign settlers in Dyfed and Ceredigion. Early the following year he took Narberth Castle by surprise, then attacked Llandovery Castle, but failed to take the tower.

The *Red Book of Hergest* version of the *Brut y Tywysogion* states that Gruffudd 'sent his companions to attack and alarm a castle that was at Abertawe which belonged to Harry Beaumont. After burning the bailey, and after the garrison had saved the tower, and after a few of his men had been killed, he withdrew'. The *Peniarth ms 20* account is similar in that Gruffudd 'sent his companions to attack a castle which Earl Henry, who was called Beaumont, had at Abertawe, but achieved nought because of the garrison except the burning of the bailey, and they withdrew after some of them had been slain'. Bearing in mind the possible strength of the garrison it is likely that Gruffudd's companions may by now have numbered several hundred.

Both versions of the *Brut* include that Gruffudd was active in Gower, recording that 'A castle in Gower he burnt outright and killed many within it. William de Londres, through fear, left the castle in his charge and his cattle and men'. It is not clear whether the two sentences are connected, The castle most likely to have been attacked was either Loughor or Llandeilo Talybont as the rebel forces would have presumably entered Gower at one or other of the fords near the two castles. However, the castle enfeoffed to William de Londres was that at Oystermouth, and if the two sentences are connected, then this would appear to have been the castle to have been attacked.

Gruffudd's attack on Gower was a temporary set-back for the Normans, but when he returned 20 years later he sparked off a revolt that led to the re-establishment of part of his father's kingdom and nearly two centuries of incessant warfare.[1]

In a charter dated 1195, Richard I confirmed several earlier grants to the Abbey of St. Taurin at Evreux in Normandy, one of which (undated) states: 'Henry, earl of Warwick, who, for the souls of Lord King William and Queen Matilda, and to himself, gave in Wales, the Church of St. Cenydd and lands for two ploughs in the vicinity of the Church, and the tithes of the vill, a suitable site for a mill, and enough of his woods for all the needs of the brethren, the tithe of rents there, and of his hunting and fishing and all his demesne; [he also gave] the Church of Tauin [possibly the ruined church at Knelston] and the Church of Pennard with their tithes, and the Church of the Isle [Burry Holms] free of all claims'. The abbey was to benefit by having Prior's Town, the most easterly part of the present-day parish of Llangenydd as an ecclesiastical manor; the tithes due to the churches of St. Taurin and Pennard; that is, one tenth of the annual produce of the land or labour (in those days a tax for the support of the Church and the clergy); and the hermitage on Burry Holms.

To exploit the manor of Prior's Town the prelates of St. Taurin appear to have ousted the Welsh clergy, replacing them with French-speaking Benedictine monks headed by a prior. This must have upset the locals; it certainly upset Urban, bishop of Llandaff, for he was soon complaining to the pope about the appropriation of church property, the land and income of which Harry, and other Marcher lords, had generously given to foreign abbeys.

A century or so later, Gerald uses the lewd and wanton behaviour of the monks at Llangenydd as an example of the degeneracy of monastic institutions. The remains of their supposed den of iniquity—the priory—lie beneath the farm adjoining the south side of the present-day church, the earliest part of which is probably no earlier than the 13th century.

Connected with the priory is the hermitage on the Island of Burry Holms. Excavations on the lower, eastern end of the island between 1965-8 revealed the existence of a stone-built, 12th century church, the largest part of which, the nave, proved to be 5.33m long by 3.42m wide, with a doorway in the south wall. The church was surrounded by a cashel—a rubble wall—and beyond the wall other buildings, including a hall and a school, were erected in the 12th to 14th centuries.

It is generally accepted that Harry Beaumont died in 1119, although a later countess of Warwick, in her pedigree of the de Newburgh family, claims that his death occurred in 1123.

CHAPTER III
Struggle for Possession

Harry Beaumont's widow, Margaret, appears to have held Gower by right of dower until at least 1156 because, in that year, she granted the vill of Llanmadog to the Order of Knights Templars. It is unlikely that Margaret ever came to Gower—the journey would have been considered too hazardous for a woman of her standing—and the wording of her grant makes it plain that she had it drafted whilst residing at the family estate of Newburgh in Normandy.

Harry Beaumont's eldest son, Roger, succeeded to the earldom of Warwick and is described as one who little affected military employment, is praised for his gentle and delightful nature, his abounding patience, yet criticized as being a weak man, more addicted to pleasure than gifted with courage. Between 1130-35 he granted land to Neath Abbey from his mother's demesne of Pennard, which suggest that he administered the lordship of Gower on his mother's behalf. The lordship had already suffered an attack in 1116, but the Welsh of Gower and West Wales were not the only ones to give men such as Roger a headache.

A papal Bull dated 16 October 1119 was given to Urban, bishop of Llandaff, in response to his grievances against the Marcher lords of south-east Wales who were appropriating church property, thereby depriving him of the land, tithes, oblations and burials of the appropriated properties. The pope saw fit to mention in his Bull numerous church properties, six of which can be located in Gower: St. Teilo de Llanferwallt (Bishopston), Llancynwalan (location uncertain, probably Rhosili), Llandeilo Porthtulon (possibly St. Peter's Well in the Caswell Valley), Llandeilo Talybont (near Pontardulais), Llangemei (Llangenydd), Cilcynhin (exact location unknown).

That same day Pope Calixtus II wrote letters to several Marcher lords warning them of the consequences of plundering church property, and ordering them to return the properties without delay, but the wrangle continued, despite a concord of 1126 in which Urban and Robert Consul, earl of Gloucester and lord of Glamorgan, came to an agreement. Among the witnesses to the concord were Roger, earl of Warwick, and the Marcher barons, Payn de Turberville, lord of Coety, and Maurice de Londres, lord of Ogmore (his father, William, had obviously died by then).

On 9 April 1128 the pope, now Honorius II, wrote a similar warning to named barons, one of whom was Maurice de Londres. In 1131 a third pope had to issue yet another Bull because Urban had complained that de Turberville's steward, Rabel, had violently ejected him from his possessions in the vill of St. Teilo de Llanferwallt.

Urban needed to raise finance for his pet project, the building of a new cathedral at Llandaff. Already, in 1119, he had laid claim to territories in the neighbouring dioceses of St. Davids and Hereford, basing his claim on the enlarged see of his predecessor, Herewald, who had benefitted from the conquests of one Caradog ap Gruffudd between 1072 and 1081. The territories which Urban laid claim to were Gower, Kidwelly, Carnwyllion, Cantref Bychan, Ystradyw, Ewias and Erging.

On 19 April 1128, Pope Honorius II wrote to the archbishop of Canterbury ordering him to ensure that the disputed territories should be Urban's till mid-Lent 1129 when all three bishops were due to appear in Rome. Only Urban turned up. The pope duly issued a Bull granting the disputed territories to Urban; he also wrote to the archbishop of Canterbury ordering him to enforce the judgement, and to the king begging him to see that judgement would be carried out. Nevertheless, the suit dragged on until it was remitted to London (to be heard presumably by the Church authorities); on 8 February 1133 a commission decided against Urban and the disputed territories were returned to their respective dioceses, except for one small area—Bishopston. There is a 7th-century charter which refers to property which King Morgan ab Arthrwys recovered for Bishop Oudoceus of Llandaff and his successors, a gift which had been personal to his predecessor Teilo—not the Church—the reason why Llandeilo Ferwallt (Bishopston) was considered the personal property of the bishops of Llandaff. King Morgan's charter states that the property centred on a monastery dedicated to St. Cyngwr (Cunuuri in Latin), and that Merwallt was abbot there when the charter was issued. The charter also gives the bounds of the land appertaining to the monastery, which correspond (except for the later addition of Manselfield) to the present-day parish boundary of Bishopston. At an unknown date prior to the 12th century the monastery was rededicated to St. Teilo whilst retaining the name of its earliest known abbot, Merwallt; hence, in the Bull of 1119, it is referred to as St. Teilo de Llanferwallt. There are no tangible remains of the old monastery; its location was presumably in the dell where the present-day parish church of St. Teilo now stands. (In post-conquest times the land appertaining to Bishopston was a miniature reflection of Gower as a whole. An earth and timber castle had been built at Barland, a partial ring-work on the edge of a steep slope; it has no recorded history. South of the 'Old Castle' lay the Englishry where foreign settlers worked the more fertile lands of the manor. To the north lay the Welshry, the less fertile lands reserved for the Welsh in the area around Upper Killay and Blackhills, east of Fairwood Common.)

St. Teilo's, Bishopston

Between 1114-29, Robert Consul had been gradually extending his authority beyond the Vale of Glamorgan, establishing castles at Kenfig, Aberafan and Neath—on the west bank, not the east—where he enfeoffed his constable, Richard de Granville, in the outermost bounds of his seigniory, but in 1129, Caradog ap Iestin, lord of Afan, hit back, forcing de Granville to abandon his land on the west bank and grant most of it to an abbey in Normandy. Twelve monks of the Order of Savigny arrived in 1130 to found an abbey that was to have its own part to play in the history of Gower.

Further west, Gruffudd ap Rhys, after his unsuccessful rebellion of 1116, appears to have come to terms with the king, for the *Brut y Tywysogion* states that, in 1127, Gruffudd was expelled from the land which the king had given him because his Norman neighbours had brought false accusations against him. Gruffudd again settled his differences with the king and for several years appears to have lived peaceably in Caeo, a commote in Cantref Mawr, where he bided his time, waiting for an opportunity to rebel. That opportunity came when, on 1 December 1135, Henry I died, to be succeeded by his nephew, Stephen. Florence of Worcester records that, on 1 January 1136, 'a battle was fought in Gower in which 516 men from the two armies perished, their bodies horribly dragged about the fields and devoured by wolves'.

An expanded and more reliable version of this event comes from the *Gesta Stephani* which states: 'The men it [Wales] rears are half-savage, swift of foot, always ready to shift both their habitation and their allegiance … and on King Henry's

Neath Abbey, founded in 1130, became home to white robed Cistercian monks
who held a great deal of land in the Gower peninsula

death they threw off the yoke which had been imposed by treaties, and issuing in bands from all parts … made hostile inroads in different quarters, laying waste the towns with robbery, fire and sword, destroying houses and butchering the population. The first object of their attack was the district of Gower … and hemming in the knights and foot soldiers, who to the number of 516 were collected in one body, they put them all to the sword'.

In his *Itinerary Through Wales*, Gerald provides further details when he recalls that, after leaving Abertawe, he made his way towards the River Loughor, 'through the plains in which Hywel ap Maredudd of Brycheiniog destroyed the English of those parts in pitched battle'. The 'plains' were probably Garn Goch Common, a location that would have been ideal for a pitched battle, something the Welsh usually avoided, which raises the question, why should Hywel offer battle to the English of Gower when his immediate enemies were the Norman lords of Brycheiniog? Did he march into Gower in support of Gruffudd ap Rhys, knowing that the king had issued orders for the troublesome Gruffudd to be brought to heel? There is no reference to Gruffudd's presence at the scene of carnage, but he certainly took advantage of the situation in the months that were to follow.

With West Wales in a state of lawlessness, Gruffudd had set his sights on Kidwelly Castle, then held by Maurice de Londres on behalf of Roger, bishop of Salisbury. Monks who saw him as their benefactor described Maurice as one who excelled in valiantness and liberality, whereas Gerald depicts him as a gullible and cruel man. Gruffudd, according to Gerald, rode north to solicit the aid of the kings of Gwynedd, and while he was away his wife, Gwenllian, marched on Kidwelly Castle, only to be defeated and captured by Maurice who put her to death along with many of her followers.

The kings of Gwynedd invaded Ceredigion in the summer and, with the aid of Hywel ap Maredudd, burned several castles. In October they invaded Ceredigion a second time with a train of about 6,000 foot soldiers and 2,000 mailed horsemen. They were supported by Gruffudd ap Rhys, Hywel ap Maredudd and Madoc ab Idnerth—at last Welsh kings were co-operating against their common enemy.

What followed bears the hallmark of another pitched battle, one that had been proposed beforehand and fought on chosen ground, because all the Marcher lords between the estuaries of the Nedd and the Dyfi assembled near Cardigan Castle. The battle which followed proved so fierce that the Normans lost 3,000 men, the survivors taking refuge in Cardigan Castle, after which the kings of Gwynedd returned home with an abundance of captives and spoils.

The kings of Gwynedd marched south again in 1137, taking several castles, Carmarthen among them. Then disaster struck: Gruffudd was slain through the treachery of his wife—his second wife presumably—and over the next few years several Welsh kings were killed in action, fighting among themselves, while Hywel ap Maredudd was slain by his own men. What had started with a success in Gower, followed by a crushing victory outside Cardigan, ended with disappointing reverses, the Normans slowly recovering lost ground.

The missing cartulary of Neath Abbey is said to have recorded that Gower was ravaged after the Battle of Garn Goch. It is possible that Hywel ap Maredudd annexed it, for the missing cartulary also stated that Gower was reconquered by Harry Beaumont's youngest son, Henry de Newburgh II, otherwise known as Henry de Warwick. His successful march on Gower must have taken place before the latter half of 1138 because, by then, the Welsh revolt had subsided and England was in a state of civil war. Henry's brother, Roger, earl of Warwick, supported King Stephen's right to rule, whereas the Marcher lords of south-east Wales, and the magnates of England's most westerly provinces, supported the claim to succession of the Empress Matilda (the daughter of King Henry I); thus a band of hostile territory lay between Warwick Castle and Gower.

Once in control of his mother's dower, Henry soon found himself cut off from the more prosperous parts of England; consequently, there was a shortage of coins with which to trade. So Henry, like other Marcher lords, minted his own currency, for in 1980, near Cardiff, a hoard of over a hundred coins was unearthed, ten of which bore various abbreviations of Sweynesse (Swansea), the name of the borough as it appeared in a charter of c.1170. The earliest coins also bear the name of (king) Stephen; the others, dating from about 1141, bear the name of HENRICI de NOVEB (Newburgh). The view that Gower had been recovered by Henry before 1141 is supported by a charter of Maurice de Londres concerning Oystermouth Church.

Sweyn's Ey (Swansea)

The name Sweyn was once a common Norse name, and the word 'Ey' is believed to mean island or inlet, a description well suited for a settlement at the mouth of the River Tawe. This has led many to believe that Swansea originated as a Norse settlement as far back as the 10th century. Unfortunately, there is absolutely no evidence to support this view, only the name spelt in a variety of ways. Norse place-names abound in Wales, almost all of them coastal locations, which suggests that names such as Sweynesse and Burry Holms were used as navigational reference points by Norse seamen, especially those from Ireland.

Despite their fearsome reputation as raiders and, in the 11th century, as mercenaries employed by Welsh kings, the Norsemen who had settled in Ireland were, by and large, farmers and traders, many of them living in or near settlements such as Dublin, Wexford and Limerick, townships which their forefathers had founded. There is no hard evidence to support their trading activities in the Bristol Channel until after 1170, the year in which adventurers from South Wales made a landing at Wexford that led to the conquest of Ireland. A late 12th-century list of the citizens of Dublin shows that two of those named were also citizens of Sweynesse, both of

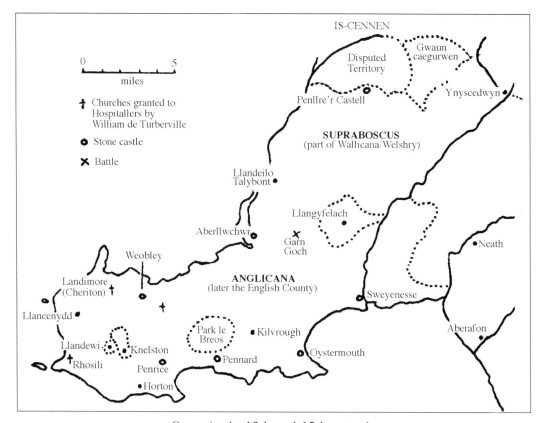

Gower in the 12th and 13th centuries

whom, it is claimed, bore Norse names: Godafridus and Ricardius filius (son of) Segeri. It has been suggested that, like so many other merchants from Bristol, the south-west of England and South Wales, they subsequently took on dual citizenship to take advantage of the trading opportunities which resulted from Henry II's charter of 1172 to the citizens of Dublin.

Abertawe was, and still is, a prime site for mercantile activity. Coins and pottery found in Wind Street and Castle Street point to the existence of a small settlement in Roman times, after which there is a hiatus in our knowledge until the *Brut* states that, in 1116, there was a castle at Abertawe which belonged to Harry Beaumont, one that was large enough to attract merchants, tradesmen and innkeepers to cater for the soldiers' needs. In time some of these entrepreneurs also engaged in commerce which had little to do with the garrison and points to the existence, close to the castle, of a borough named Sweynesse. Perhaps Sweyn was one of the earliest and most influential merchant to settle in the shadows of the castle.

The Sons of Gruffudd ap Rhys

Welsh rulers saw themselves as kings, but by the 12th century the chroniclers considered it prudent to speak of them as princes (*tywysogion*). When Gruffudd ap Rhys died, leaving four sons, they were all princes, exceptional in that the *Brut* mentions no hostility between them. After Anarawd, the eldest, had been slain in 1143, the remaining princes—Cadell, the second eldest; Maredudd, born in 1130; Rhys, born *c*.1132—pursued their war against the Normans. The Marcher lords of West Wales were powerless to stop them, unable to draw upon support because of the civil war in England.

In 1151, Cadell was left for half-dead after being severely bruised, whilst hunting, by some of the men of Tenby. Maredudd and Rhys assembled a host, made for Gower and laid siege to the castle of Aberllwchwr (Loughor), burning it to the ground and ravaging the land. The two events appear to be connected, though why Maredudd and Rhys should make for Gower when the men who attacked their brother were from Tenby is unclear.

Excavation at Loughor has revealed that a ring-bank, surmounted by a palisade, had surrounded the level summit of a mound. A wooden gate-tower may have occupied the western end of the mound, the first floor serving as living quarters. To the east, the excavators could point to the remains of a timber kitchen, open on the west side, that had been destroyed in a fire, and to a cobbled path that had led to the vestige of an oven set in the ring-bank. It is likely that, at the time of the siege, the castle was held by Henry de Vilers, the same who granted the land of Cwrt y Carnau to Neath Abbey. It is also possible that de Vilers died in the attack because, in a confirmation charter of 1230, it is Henry de Warwick who made the following gifts to the Hospitallers: 'in Gower, of the gift of Henry de Newburgh, the church of Loughor [St. Michaels] with all its appurtenances and liberties, and in the vill of the same name one burgage [a plot of land on which a town house could be built] with

The Orders of Knights Templars and Hospitallers of St. John

The Order of Knights Templars had been established about 1118 by a small band of knights to protect pilgrims on their way to the Holy Land. Adopting the Benedictine rule, many young nobles joined the Order, conspicuous for their white mantles bearing a large, Red Cross. In time the Templars became wealthy and powerful through gifts of land and money, so much so that they became the bankers of Europe, which in turn made them unpopular. Then, in 1307, the Order was charged with heresy; many of its members were tortured, the Grand Master and others burned at the stake, and much of the Order's possessions passed to the Hospitallers.

The Hospitallers, otherwise known as the Knights Hospitallers of St. John (the Baptist) of Jerusalem, was another military, religious order. It was founded about 1048 when a group of merchants secured permission to build a hospital in Jerusalem for sick and infirm pilgrims. The hospital was supervised by Benedictine monks who wore black habits bearing a white, Maltese cross. The Order had its first Grand Master in 1118, after which it took on a military aspect, its members pledged to chastity, obedience and to support Christianity to the death. However, with the wane of a crusading spirit, the Order declined until, in this country, it was suppressed by King Henry VIII in 1540. The French revolution proved a death-blow to the Order on the Continent.

another burgage in the vill of Sweynesse'. The above entry indicates there were two boroughs in Gower—Aberllwchwr and Sweynesse—and that Aberllwchwr was, at one time, in the hands of de Warwick, suggesting that either de Vilers died without an heir, in which case his fief would have escheated to the Countess Margaret, or that his heir was a minor and therefore the heir and the fief had been placed under the wardship of de Warwick until such time as the heir was 21.

But why did Henry de Warwick—the man who had reconquered Gower—not raise the siege of Aberllwchwr? The answer may be that his hold on Gower was fairly tenuous, for two years later, in May 1153, Morgan ap Caradog, lord of Afan, stormed and burnt Aberafan Castle with the support of Maredudd and Rhys. To have achieved this they must have marched through Gower—without meeting opposition it seems—confident that their lines of communication would not be severed. This implies that, after the attack on Aberllwchwr, Henry de Warwick considered it expedient to collude with Maredudd and Rhys, but whatever the intrigue, Aberllwchwr was rebuilt, the gate-house/hall apparently in stone—the scant remains of this tower should not be confused with the later stone tower visible today. Two timber buildings were raised within the ring-bank, one on the north, one on the east.

Henry's brother, Roger, earl of Warwick, died on 12 June 1153, and the honour of Warwick passed to Roger's son, William. The succession did not affect Henry's position as heir to Gower, nor his position as custodian of Gower while his mother lived; this is evidenced by a charter in which his mother, Margaret, granted the vill of Llanmadog to the Order of Knights Templars:

> Margaret, countess of Warwick, to William, earl of Warwick, and all the barons of that honour, and the barons of Gower, saluting. Be it known that I have dedicated to the Church of St. Mary [in the town of Warwick] of the knights of the Temple of Jerusalem which is called the Temple of Solomon of Jerusalem, the vill of Llanmadog, with all its appurtenances … by the assent of Henry, my son, who is heir to this land [Gower] wholly and quietly and free of all secular service. Witnesses, etc. Given in the 1156 year of the incarnation of our Lord, at the Chapter of St. Stephen, in Normandy, next to Newburgh.

In Gower William de Turberville had donated the churches of Rhosili, Landimore and Llanrhidian with its subsidiary chapel of Walterston to the Hospitallers. Other benefactors gave the churches of Penmaen, Ilston, Capel Ieuan, Loughor and Penrice; finally, in 1307, the Order took possession of the church and vill of Llanmadog.

In 1153 Cadell, who had never fully recovered from the attack made upon him by the men of Tenby, went on pilgrimage, leaving everything in the hands of his younger brothers. Two years later, Maredudd died. In the meantime Henry II had been crowned king of England. In 1158 Henry advanced into West Wales, forcing Rhys to submit and Ceredigion, Ystrad Tywi and part of Dyfed—the gains of over 20 years of fighting—were taken from him. All that he had left was Cantref Mawr and a promise of another cantref, a promise that materialized in the form of a few scattered vills.

Not to be humiliated, Rhys attacked and burnt all the castles in Ceredigion, bringing Henry back once more to Wales, and Rhys was forced to gave him hostages. When Rhys invaded Ceredigion again in 1164, all the princes of North and central Wales joined the revolt. In response Henry summoned troops from all over England, from Scotland, Normandy, Anjou, Aquitaine and Poitou, and mercenaries were hired from Flanders. Henry moved into North Wales, but the weather disrupted his plans, leaving Rhys free to regain his former possessions.

Events were soon to change the relationship between Henry and Rhys. In August 1170, Richard Strongbow, earl of Pembroke, sailed to Ireland on a private expedition that had the king's blessing, becoming king of Leinster the following spring. In December the same year, Thomas Becket, archbishop of Canterbury, was murdered by knights who mistakenly believed they were acting in the king's interest. Strongbow's rise to kingship was seen by Henry as a challenge to his authority, whereas Becket's murder left him in need of friends—and he sought one of these in Rhys. *En route* to Ireland to claim his overlordship of Strongbow's conquests, Henry met Rhys and acknowledged his gains in West Wales. Even more

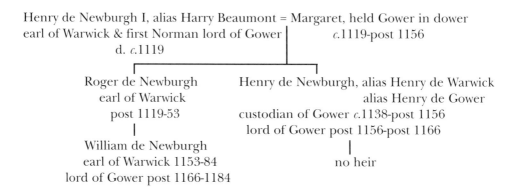

Henry de Newburgh I, alias Harry Beaumont = Margaret, held Gower in dower
earl of Warwick & first Norman lord of Gower | *c.*1119-post 1156
d. *c.*1119

Roger de Newburgh · · · Henry de Newburgh, alias Henry de Warwick
earl of Warwick · · · alias Henry de Gower
post 1119-53 · · · custodian of Gower *c.*1138-post 1156
· · · lord of Gower post 1156-post 1166
William de Newburgh
earl of Warwick 1153-84 · · · no heir
lord of Gower post 1166-1184

The de Newburgh Family Tree

surprising, when he returned from Ireland in 1172, he appointed Rhys justiciar of South Wales, giving him power over Welshmen and Normans alike. Henceforth he would be known as the Lord Rhys. He was no longer a threat to Gower, and peace and prosperity were in the wind.

Earl William's Charter

It is not known when Henry de Warwick inherited his mother's dower, but in the *Liber Rubeus*, which lists the fiefs that were subject to Earl William in 1166, he appears as the holder of Gower under the name of Henry de Gower due to his long absence from Warwick, and possibly to avoid confusion with another Henry de Newburgh, a relative. This is the last we hear of Henry and, at an unknown date, he must have died childless because Gower escheated to his nephew, William, earl of Warwick (see family tree above). William, like his father and grandfather before him, appears to have been a pious, mild-tempered man who little affected military employment. About 1170 he was obliged to issue a charter to the burgesses of Sweynesse, possibly in response to complaints of malpractice by his officers.

As a class the burgesses had been growing in numbers and in wealth for over a hundred years. For an annual rent of one shilling they each held a plot of land, a burgage, within the town without any obligation to work the land, or perform castle guard. In Wales they had to be induced to settle in areas that were subject to periodic attacks; they also required their privileges in writing in case of dispute:

> Be it known to you all, both French and English, present and future, that I [William] have granted, and by my charter confirmed, to the burgesses of Sweynesse these customs, that is to say, to every burgess a burgage with all its appurtenances, to wit, their assarts [the right to create clearings, to cultivated forest waste] and to everyone seven acres beyond the wood [north of Sweynesse] and above Burlakesbroke [Burlais Brook, a stream which rose near Cockett Station and flowed to Cwmbwrlais, later Cwmbwrla, to join the Tawe River near High Street Station], and pasture as far as Hackedewey [meaning a

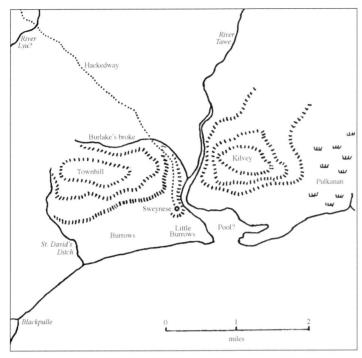

Places mentioned in Earl William's charter c.1170. The area bounded by St. David's Ditch, Burlakesbroke, the Tawe and the sea later became known as the Town and Franchise of Sweynesse

way with gates, now Pentregethin Road, which led to what later became known as the Portmead, the lord's meadow, a large tract of grazing land, stretching from the present-day district of Portmead to Waun-arlwydd] and as far as the Lyu [either the rivers Lliw or Llan] and as far as St. David's Ditch [the Brynmill Stream which rose to the north of Hill House and fell to the sea below Singleton Park], and in such a manner as none may have any easement [right of way] there except myself and the aforesaid burgesses; and the woods on all side about my borough to pasture their herds as far as they can go in a day and return the same night to their homes; and they may have their swine in my woods, freely and quietly without custom; oak to make their houses and fences and ships, rendering for a ship twelve pence, and all other wood for their fire and for their easement; and to carry and sell whatever they shall wish and can.

They may have without hindrance all wild beasts of my woods which they can take, except the stag and hind and wild boar and marten. And moreover I have granted to them within Pulkanan and Blackpulle [between Crymlyn Burrows and Blackpill] all the beach upon which to make their fisheries. And if it happens that porpoise or sturgeon be taken in any such fishery, it is mine, and I will give him to whom the fishery belongs twelve pence, or one load of corn. And if the burgesses can take fish in any manner outside the pool [possibly a small bay at the mouth of Tawe later to be known as Fabian's Bay] it shall be theirs. And if when the tide ebbs they shall find wreck without the pool, it shall be half mine and half theirs. And if they shall find wreck on dry land it shall be all mine.

And whenever my men-at-arms shall take grass [collect fodder] for my horses, my burgesses likewise may take with them, except in my meadows. And if I shall summon my burgesses to arms, or to any business of mine, they shall go at their own expense if so be that they can return to their homes the same night. And if I shall lead them further, they shall be at my expense. And if they shall enrich themselves, they may have half against me.

And I have granted peace in their homes, and outside their houses for the space of seven feet of the ground before their doors; and on their burgages an oven, brewhouse and household stuff, and all their profits, freely and quietly. And if a burgess shall incur a forfeiture [commit a crime] and shall be brought into my court[a] by view of his neighbours and not have bail by pledges [material things given as security] and sureties [persons who will take responsibility for him], then he shall plead in my court, and if he shall have bail by pledges and sureties before he shall be brought into my court, he shall plead in his hundred court. A burgess must not plead elsewhere than in the hundred court when he is challenged of [charged with] treason of my body or of my town. And if a burgess shall be challenged of this treason, he shall purge [atone] himself by oath with five others, unless I shall have aught to say thereon beforehand. My justice shall not implead [prosecute] a burgess without a burgess as a witness. It is not permissible for any of my household to witness against a burgess.

He who shall shed blood from noon on Saturday to Monday morning [shall pay] forty shillings for forfeiture; and from Monday morning to noon on Saturday [shall pay] twelve pence for forfeiture, except it be premeditated assault and forestallage.[b] No foreign merchant may cut cloths by retail, nor buy skins, nor hides, except of a burgess.

If a burgess wishes to depart and sells his burgage and gives away his house, he shall pay four pence to the Toll-collector,[c] and let him quit; and if he cannot sell his house, let him do his will with what is above the ground. And if a burgess goes away upon his business, let him deliver his house to someone to render his rights, and let him go and return when he shall wish as to his own.

The aforesaid privileges I have granted to my burgesses of Sweynesse and to their heirs, to hold of me and my heirs by hereditary right, at a rent from each one of them to me, each year, of twelve pence. And that this grant be firm and inviolable, I have brought these to be witnesses: William de Londres, etc.

---

[a]There were two courts: the lord's court and the hundred court, both held at Sweynesse. The justices of the hundred court were the burgesses themselves, and provided the accused could obtain bail by pledges and sureties, then he would be tried by his peers in the hundred court. The clauses in this paragraph suggest that there had been friction between the burgesses and their lord—perhaps their previous lord, Henry de Warwick—which Earl William sought to rectify.

[b]Forestallage occurred when an outsider offered goods for sale on better terms to people as they approached the town. It was considered a serious offence by the burgesses who claimed a monopoly on trade, and to protect their interests further they prohibited foreign merchants from cutting cloths for retail, or buying skins and hides from anyone other than a Sweynesse burgess. Gerald informs us that towns such as Sweynesse had frequently to import corn and salt, and the Pipe Rolls of 1188 refer to imports from the West of England of corn and bacon for provisioning the castle of Sweynesse.

[c]The Toll-collector was a burgess appointed to collect money from his peers on behalf of Earl William - another example of how the burgesses took control over their affairs. They distrusted their lord and his officers, seeing them as potentially extortionate; they distrusted the Welsh, too, which is why, in the 12th century, no Welshmen would have been allowed to live in the town let alone own a burgage.

Gower Becomes Crown Property

William de Newburgh died in the Holy Land on 15 November 1184, and Gower became Crown property. William had pledged the lordship as security for a loan of £44 from a Jew, Bruno of London, and King Henry took the opportunity to cancel the debt, deducting it from a huge fine of 2,000 marks which Bruno had to render to the Crown, so acquiring the land. Gower remained Crown property for some 18 years, until February 1203 when King John granted it to William de Breos lll.

In 1187 Christendom became alarmed by news that the Saracens had taken Jerusalem, and in March 1188, Baldwin, archbishop of Canterbury, accompanied by Gerald, entered Wales via Hereford to preach the Third Crusade. A Norman by birth, Gerald has been described as tall and handsome, ambitious, haughty, sarcastic, quick-witted, eloquent, a man who loved to show off. Educated at St. Davids, St. Peter's Abbey, Gloucester and the University of Paris, he could speak several languages, yet could not speak Welsh, at least, not fluently. At the age of 28 he became archdeacon of Brecon and subsequently a royal chaplain.

Archbishop Baldwin and Gerald zigzagged their way south to Newport, then headed west through the Vale of Glamorgan. At Margam, Morgan ap Caradog, lord of Afan, offered to guide them through his territory as far as the west bank of the River Nedd. 'We set off once more,' Gerald writes, 'and encountered the twin hazards of a sandy shore and an incoming tide, then crossed the ford over the River Afan … As we approached the Nedd [near Briton Ferry], which is the most dangerous of all rivers to cross on account of the quicksand which immediately engulfs anything placed upon it, one of the packhorses, the only one possessed by me, was almost sucked into the abyss … Eventually it was pulled out with difficulty, thanks to the efforts of our servants who risked their lives in doing so, and not without some damage to books and baggage. Ignoring the advice of Morgan, so scared were we, we hurried where caution should have prevailed and eventually crossed the river by boat as the ford changed with the tide and cannot be located after heavy rain'.

On the west bank they passed the hill-fort of Hen Gastell, thence over the Crymlyn Burrows. Gerald does not relate how they crossed the Tawe—presumably it was by boat—but does say that they spent the night at the Castle de Sweynsei or Sweineshe (Gerald's spelling), a place which the Welsh called *Abertau*.

The following morning, when people assembled after mass, many were induced to join the crusade, Baldwin marking them with the sign of the Cross. Among those to come forward was an aged Welshman named Cador who, after bemoaning his years, fell at the archbishop's feet, offering one tenth of his estate for the service of the Cross. Cador wept bitterly, entreating from Baldwin the remission of half a penance, which Baldwin granted, but after a while Cador returned and said, 'My lord, as I have a firm inclination to undertake the journey [to the Holy Land] I request a remission of the remaining part of my penance and, in addition to my former gift, I will equal the sum from the residue of my tenths.' Gerald tells us that, smiling, Baldwin embraced the man with admiration.

That night, in the archbishop's private room, two monks were discussing the events of their journey when one said, 'This is a hard province, brother.' The other, referring to the quicksand, replied, 'And yet yesterday it was found too soft.'

Gerald's journey continued round the coastal regions of Wales and thence via Chester back to Hereford, by which time, Gerald claims, about 3,000 men had taken the Cross—not all Welshmen, but also Flemings, French and Saxons who had settled in Wales. Unfortunately, by the time the Crusade got under way many of the volunteers had changed their minds. Even Gerald, who was in his early forties at the time, obtained a dispensation from the pope on the grounds of poverty, age and physical weakness—though he lived to a then ripe old age of 77.

Gerald relates that most of the Welsh he encountered in his travels were pastoralists, tending cattle, sheep and goats. They also grew oats and, where possible, barley and wheat; also hay, flax and vegetables such as leeks and cabbages. He suggests they paid no attention to commerce, shipping or manufacture.

Llangyfelach Church tower, with the church separate in the background

The Welsh, Gerald claimed, showed a greater respect than other nations to churches, clerics, the relics of saints, holy books and the Cross; hence their churches enjoyed exceptional tranquillity. Where Gower is concerned these claims are borne out by the bard, Gwynfardd Brycheiniog, who, in the early 13th century, speaks of the stately church at Llangyfelach where there is 'happiness and great devotion'.

Although lavish in his praise for the Welsh, Gerald did not shrink from publicizing their faults, declaring that they were a people quick to action, more stubborn in a bad cause than a good one, having no scruples about taking a false oath for the sake of temporary gain; they considered it right to commit acts of plunder, theft and robbery not only against foreigners, but even against their own kind. One bad habit was that of moving or digging up boundary marks and placing them further afield in order to acquire more land; another was the custom of partitionable inheritance in which property was divided equally between sons. Yet another trait which

Gerald found fault with was that brothers showed more affection to one another when dead, claiming that while they lived they constantly quarrelled, even fought, but if anyone dared to interfere, or if someone killed one of the brothers, then the other brothers would go to great lengths to avenge the deceased.

At the time of Gerald's visit to Sweynesse Castle, William de Londres was seneschal. The Pipe Rolls record a payment in 1188 of £6 made for nine baskets of grain delivered to William for the keeping of Sweynesse Castle; also 45 shillings (£2.25) for 40 sides of bacon. The previous year an entry reads: 'to William de Londres – 20 marks [a mark being two-thirds of a pound] for repairs to the king's castle of Sweynesse on the instructions of Ranulf de Granville'. These repairs were probably routine.

Henry II died on 6 July 1189; his son, Richard I, had no sooner ascended to the throne than he found himself at odds with the Lord Rhys, whose response was to overrun southern Pembrokeshire, Carnwyllion and Gower, capturing Laugharne and Llanstephan before besieging Carmarthen. Gerald was sent for to act as a mediator, but neither Richard nor Rhys made any serious attempt at settling their differences; moreover, Richard does not appear to have been sufficiently alarmed by the situation to be diverted from travelling to the Middle East.

In 1190, with Richard on Crusade, the Lord Rhys wasted no time in launching a second campaign, taking several castles in the process, Kidwelly being one of them. William de Breos IV was seneschal of Gower that year—he held it from September 1189 to 1191—and the Pipe Rolls record a payment that same year for the hire of ships and sailors for carrying provisions to Carmarthen and Sweynesse.

Entries for 1192 are more numerous, and include £10 to de Londres for custody of Sweynesse Castle; £16.13s.8d to Nicholas Avene at Bristol for preparing ships for war and sending them to Sweynesse; 100 loads of grain valued at £10 to de Londres for keeping the castle; half a mark to Henry fitzElye, courier, for bringing the king's instructions about Sweynesse Castle. These entries point to trouble, details of which are given in the *Annales Cambriae*, which states that, in the latter half of 1192, 'Rhys … led his host towards Abertawe and besieged the town for 10 weeks, and the townspeople would have surrendered through starvation had it not been for the dissension between Rhys's sons which forced him to abandon the siege after some of his men had been drowned the previous day'.

There is reason to believe that the feudal host mustered at Gloucester, and that there may even have been skirmishing around the beleaguered town because an entry in the Pipe Rolls refers to a Northampton knight, Hugh de Villiers, being reimbursed for the loss of a horse, valued at £2, which died near Sweynesse in the king's service. No further action appears to have been taken against Rhys until Herbert Walter was made justiciar of South Wales in 1193, but in 1196 Rhys launched yet another offensive, this time into central Wales. It proved short-lived, for the following year an outbreak of yellow plague carried off a large number of people, including Rhys.

There are many gaps in records of 12th-century Gower, and nothing exemplifies this more than the number of occasions in which Gower *Anglicana* suffered at the hands of the Welsh and the sources from which the information is obtained. The *Brut*, for example, records that Gower sustained incursions from West Wales in 1116, 1151 and 1189, but makes no mention of any other attack. The *Annales Cambriae*, by comparison, records the ten-week siege of Sweynesse, but has nothing to say about the incursions mentioned in the *Brut*. Neither the *Brut* nor the *Annales* have anything to say about the battle between Sweynesse and Loughor in 1136, knowledge of which comes from English sources. The fact that the records are fragmented, in many cases the product of chance, strongly suggests that there must have been a number of unrecorded attacks. Confusingly, in the following century the monks at Neath Abbey complained that their holdings in Gower were of little value because whenever a lord of Gower died the lordship was overrun. There is no evidence to support this view, only that Gower was overrun in 1136, following the death of King Henry I, and again in 1189 after the death of Henry II who had, indeed, been lord of Gower.

As to the native Welsh of Gower, there is no evidence that they rallied in support of any incursions from West Wales, or that they rebelled whenever they had a grievance against the Norman lords of Gower. Evidence of their rebellious inclinations do not appear in the records until the late 13th century. While the Welsh can be admired for their dogged resistance, tribute also has to be paid to the tenacity of the settlers, several times smitten by pestilences, their lands overrun, their homes burnt, many of them killed or led away into miserable captivity, above all suffering the loss of 516 men on or near Garn Goch Common. Yet they persisted in the face of hardship.

The Lord Rhys had made arrangements for his hard-won kingdom to pass undivided to his eldest son, Gruffudd, but it was not to be. Another son, Maelgwn, took Gruffudd prisoner and the kingdom of Deheubarth ceased to exist, being shared between Maelgwn and his brothers, Rhys Gryg and Maredudd. Gruffudd's two sons, Rhys Ieuanc and Owain, were excluded from the division of land and do not seem to have acquired territory until 1201 when, on the death of their uncle Maredudd, they seized his lordship of Cantref Bychan, by which time Gower had entered a new phase in its history.

CHAPTER IV
King John and the de Breoses

On the death of Richard 1 his younger brother, John, entered Rouen and had himself invested as duke of Normandy on 25 April 1199. Crossing the Channel, he arrived at Shoreham on 25 May, determined to be crowned king of England—but there was a problem: Richard had named his nephew, Arthur, the son of another brother, Geoffrey of Britanny, who had died in 1186, as his heir.

John, however, had in his train one William de Breos, a baron known to have been in attendance on Richard on the day prior to his death, who claimed that, while he lay dying, Richard had declared that John should succeed him and not Arthur. Whatever the truth the majority of barons were persuaded to accept de Breos's claim and, on 27 May, John was crowned king at Westminster, and so also became lord of Gower.

The name Breos, or Braose, comes from Briouze-Saint-Gervais, a village near Falaise in Normandy. On the English side of the Channel the name first appears in 1073 when a William de Breos I attested a grant as the first lord of Bramber, a rich lordship in Sussex, which may have been his reward for his (unproven) part in the Battle of Hastings in 1066. William de Breos I was certainly favoured by the king, for in the *Domesday Survey* of 1086-7 it is apparent that, apart from Bramber, he held 56 other lordships in England. He was succeeded by his son, Philip, who, about 1093, availed himself of Radnor on the border of Wales, which made him a Marcher lord. From Radnor he invaded the neighbouring Welsh districts of Builth and Elfael.

In the 1130s, Philip was succeeded by his eldest son, William II, who married Bertha, daughter of Milo, earl of Hereford. On the death of Bertha's brother, Bertha and her two sisters became co-heiresses of their father's huge estate, a windfall which resulted in William II becoming lord of both Brecknock and Abergavenny. By 1175 William II's eldest son, William III, had become lord of Brecknock, and it was he who supported John's claim to the throne.

Churchmen praised William III for his piety, mindful no doubt of his donations to the Church, but there was another side to his character. In 1175 he summoned Seisyll ap Dyfnwal, the Welsh lord of Upper Gwent, along with leading Welshmen of

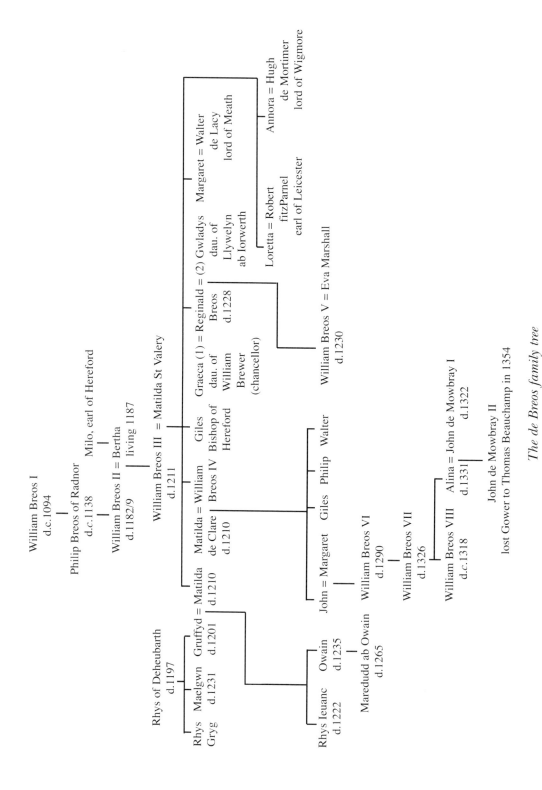

The de Breos family tree

the area to a banquet at his castle of Abergavenny. While his Welsh guests were seated at table, William III read out a royal ordinance to the effect that no traveller should carry a bow or any other unlawful weapon. William knew that no Welshman would comply with such a demand, and no sooner had his guests expressed disapproval than, at a given signal, armed men rushed into the hall, and within moments Seisyll and his followers lay dead. Armed men were then dispatched to Seisyll's court where they seized his wife and murdered his seven-year-old son, Cadwaladr.

By the time of Richard's death, William III had risen to become a powerful Marcher baron, holding numerous estates in England and Wales, and was also sheriff of Hereford. The marriage arrangements of his family were no less impressive, his offspring marrying into the most powerful families in the realm, while he himself had married Matilda (or Maud) de St. Valery. Matilda proved herself to be a formidable personality, repulsing a Welsh assault on Painscastle in the Welsh borders; she bore William at least seven children.

During the early part of his reign, John was preoccupied with affairs in France. In June 1202 he was drawn into an all-out war because his nephew and Richard's proclaimed heir, Arthur, had roused the barons of north-west France to revolt and King Philip of France was only too willing to support him. On each occasion that John campaigned in France he did so with William III in close attendance. Consequently, favours were showered on William and his family; there were acquisitions too.

In January 1201, John accepted William's offer of 5,000 marks for the Honour of Limerick in Ireland. William put off paying the installments, believing that John would not press him for money. In October 1202 William gained custody of Glamorgan, Gwynllwg and Gower (The family had earlier been granted custody of Gower by Richard l, but this had lapsed in 1191). William now controlled almost the whole of south-east Wales, from Builth to the Bristol Channel, as well as a great deal of land on the English side of the border, from Ludlow to Gloucester; he also held St. Clears in west Wales which he had taken by force from the Welsh in 1194 (see map on p.49).

By the beginning of 1203 the war in France was going against John. How serious the situation had become can be judged from the circumstances in which John granted the lordship of Gower to William. Many years later a descendant of William was required to produce his title and he claimed that the charter had been made 'in Normandy in the time of war between King John and the king of France on account of de Breos threatening to depart from him and return to England, the king being terrified of the said war'.

A translation of the charter's Latin reads: 'John, by the grace of God, king of England, lord of Ireland, duke of Aquitaine and earl of Anjou, to the archbishops, etc., greetings. Know ye that we have given and granted, and by this charter confirmed to our beloved and trustworthy William de Breos, all the land of Gower ... to have and to hold ... by the service of one knight for all service ... [for a period of 40 days each year during time of war]. Given in the hand of Hugh de Wells at Rouen the 23rd day of February in the fourth year of our reign [1203]'.[1]

Despite the fact that Arthur had been captured in July 1202, John still felt threatened by his nephew's existence and was advised to pull out Arthur's eyes and castrate him; that way he could never rule nor father a child. Two men were sent to Falaise Castle where Arthur was held, but the custodian, Hubert de Burgh, refused permission for the order to be carried out. To cover up his leniency, de Burgh let it be known that the mutilation had been performed and that Arthur had died of his wounds. When word spread of Arthur's fate the whole of north-western France was roused to violent indignation, so much so that it fell to de Breos to present Arthur safe in life and limb. That was not to be so for long. Arthur was transferred to Rouen Castle where, according to the *Annales de Margam* 'after dinner on Tuesday [3 April 1203] when he [John] was drunk and possessed by the Devil, he slew Arthur with his own hand. Then, tying a heavy stone to the body, he cast it into the Seine. The body was discovered by a fisherman and dragged to the bank where it was identified as the body of Arthur; it was taken in secret for burial'.

Matters went from bad to worse for John, and by the end of June 1204 he had lost the whole of north-western France, though he still retained the huge duchy of Aquitaine to the south. The following year, William may have been numbered among the barons who refused to accompany John on an expedition to recover north-western France, which would explain why William found himself out of favour and the following year John relieved William of the custody of Glamorgan and Gwynllwg.

John also soon found himself at odds with the pope due to his refusal, in June 1207, to accept the pope's nominee for the post of archbishop of Canterbury. Frustrated by John's stance, the pope threatened to proclaim an interdict on England and Wales. Fearful that this would lead the barons to renounce their oaths of allegiance to him, in March 1208 John ordered suspect barons to hand over a son, or near relative, as a hostage. Most complied within days of the interdict being pronounced, but when John's agents demanded of William a son, William's wife, Matilda, retorted, 'I will not deliver up any son of mine to your Lord King John, not when I know he murdered his own nephew, Arthur'.

When informed of the response, John summoned William to appear before him, William excusing himself on the grounds that he was sick. On 18 April 1208, Gerard d'Athies, sheriff of the shires of Gloucester and Hereford, took steps to distrain upon William's chattels in Wales. In company with the sheriff of Shropshire, d'Athies entered William's domain at the head of 25 mounted serjeants and 500 foot soldiers. William must have known that John was harassing him with the intention of provoking armed conflict and did not respond. To increase the pressure, on 29 April, William was ordered to pay 1,000 marks within four days to cover the cost of the expedition that had been sent against him. By the end of September, William had been forced to flee to Ireland with his family.

Before the close of the year John granted away parts of the de Breos estate, but kept much of it for himself, including Gower. This is confirmed by two charters both dated 11 November 1208, one of which reads: 'The king, etc. Know ye that we have released the Welshmen of Gower from the custom which our servants of the Castle of Sweynesse have had of taking their food with the aforesaid Welshmen, and we will that thereafter they be neither molested nor aggrieved'. The charter probably refers to the custom which serjeants of the peace had of being fed and billeted whilst doing their rounds—arresting criminals, distraining debtors and carrying out the decisions of the lord's court at Sweynesse. The practice had become a grievance due to the serjeants molesting their hosts, English as well as Welsh, for an almost identical charter was addressed to the English settlers. The Pipe Rolls for 1208 suggests the charter had cost the Welshmen fifty marks and horses for the chase; they suggest, too, that the Welshmen may have been slow in parting with their money.

Under John, Gower became the responsibility of Faulkes de Bréauté, a mercenary captain with a reputation for plundering churches. Early in 1207 de Bréauté had replaced William de Breos as custodian of Glamorgan and Gwynllwg and the Pipe Rolls for 1208 record a payment to him of 100 marks for keeping Sweynesse Castle.

Early in 1210, John decided to settle affairs with William de Breos and teach the Irish barons who shielded him a lesson. John was at Sweynesse between 28 and 30 May as chancery rolls verify. One account relates that Faulkes de Bréauté was paid 50 marks for strengthening the castle, another that he was paid £8.6s.9d to provide entertainment for the king while he stayed within the castle bailey. Yet another account indicates that de Bréauté was paid £5 to cover the cost of four ships, privately owned merchantmen, commandeered to convey troops to Ireland.

Before John sailed, William appeared off the Pembrokeshire coast and through intermediaries offered an incredible 40,000 marks for the king's 'good will', but John spurned the offer, declaring there could be no terms while Matilda remained free. So William wasted the country, hoping to divert John from his purpose—to no avail. After John set sail, William remained in Wales, regaining territory.

John, meanwhile, disembarked at Crook early in June and led his host through Leinster to be met by Walter de Lacy, lord of Meath and William de Breos's son-in-law, who offered to submit without a fight, only to be dispossessed of his lands. Walter's brother, Hugh de Lacy, lord of Ulster, conducted a fighting withdrawal before fleeing to Scotland, accompanied by Matilda and members of her family. When they came ashore, Hugh de Lacy and Reginald de Breos made good their escape, but the rest of the Breoses were taken prisoner and shipped to Bristol.

Flushed with success, John arrived home to find Matilda offering to ransom herself for 40,000 marks, William turning himself in to confirm the offer, although he must have known that he could never raise such a vast sum of money. In the ascendancy, John had Matilda and her eldest son, William the Younger, transferred

Effigy of King John on his tomb at Worcester Cathedral,
as preserved in a plaster cast in the
Victoria and Albert Museum, London

to Windsor Castle where they starved to death while he waited for William to return with the ransom.

In despair, William fled for France where he died in his early sixties at Corbeil, just outside Paris, on 9 September 1211. There were many exiles at his funeral—his offspring, Giles and Loretta, and possibly Reginald. The funeral was conducted by the pope's chosen archbishop of Canterbury, Stephen Langton.

In the meantime, John had turned his attention on North Wales. Llywelyn ap Iorwerth, prince of Gwynedd, had been born in 1173 when Gwynedd had for years been fragmented between several members of the ruling dynasty. At 14 years of age he had set out to remove, one by one, those relatives whom he saw as rivals. So impressive had his rise to power been that John had singled him out for special consideration, giving him the hand in marriage of his illegitimate daughter, Joan, but John had cause to be watchful of his up-and-coming son-in-law who, by expanding beyond his borders, seemed destined to become pre-eminent among the princes of Wales. Then, in 1210, Llywelyn overstepped the mark in support, perhaps, of William de Breos. Early in 1211 John invaded North Wales, aided by the lesser princes of Wales who felt threatened by Llywelyn's rise to power. In response Llywelyn retreated to the mountains of Snowdonia. John advanced as far as Degannwy where his soldiers suffered from a shortage of food, so much so that the flesh of horses became their finest dishes; having lost many men, John returned home with little achieved.

Early in July, John tried again, leaving Oswestry with an even larger army, fully provisioned. After crossing the River Conway he sent men to torch Bangor, at which point Llywelyn sent Joan to seek whatever terms she could—and they were harsh. Llywelyn lost all his lands east of the Conway, had to pay a heavy tribute and provide 30 hostages.

With typical insensitivity John gave orders for castles to be built that were threatening to his Welsh allies, causing them to unite under Llywelyn. The trouble started at the end of June 1212 when Maelgwn and Rhys Gryg, sons of Lord Rhys, attacked and burnt the new castle at Aberystwyth. The attack was followed by Cadwallon ab Ifor Bach of Senghenydd ravaging the lowlands of Glamorgan. In July, Llywelyn joined his former enemies, all of whom received the blessing of the pope who released them from their

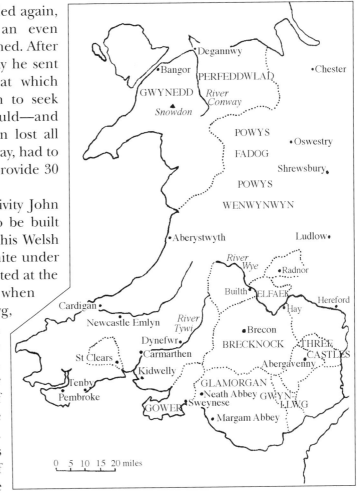

Welsh lands held in fief or in custody by the de Breos family

allegiance to the king and lifted the interdict from their lands.

John responded to the occasion, determined to finish off his son-in-law. Troops mustering for a return to France were redirected to Chester; that same month John gave orders for 28 Welsh hostages to be hanged. After watching them die, John sat down for dinner when messengers arrived, one from the king of Scotland, the other from his own daughter, Joan, both warning that, if he entered Wales, his barons would kill him in the midst of battle. John lost his nerve and called off his invasion, leaving Llywelyn free to reconquer his lost lands. Further south, Rhys Gryg burnt the town of Sweynesse, and Rhys Ieuanc made considerable gains in the lordship of Brecknock.

John had been excommunicated in 1209, but in May 1213 he came to terms with the pope in order to counter growing opposition to his rule. A clause in the settlement required that all exiles should be allowed to return home, among them William de Breos's second son, Giles, bishop of Hereford, who had every intention of restoring the family estate, and who kept in touch with disgruntled barons.

Full of surprises, John produced his trump card on 4 March 1215 when he vowed to go on crusade, effectively putting his kingdom under the protection of the Church for three years, so safeguarding it from rebellious action by his disgruntled barons. The following day, he confirmed Giles's offer of 9,000 marks for what remained of the family estate; thus Giles became a Marcher baron.

In Gower the situation proved to be somewhat different, for it had been in the hands of Faulkes de Bréauté until a writ, dated 29 January 1214, instructed him to hand it over (along with the castles of Carmarthen and Cardigan) to William Marshal, earl of Pembroke, whose loyalty lay with John. It would appear that the Anglo-Norman settlers in Gower were also prepared to support the king, with the kingdom now on the verge of civil war. Indeed, the citizens of Sweynesse were that confident that John would prevail against the rebellious barons that, about the beginning of May 1215, they sent a deputation to him to obtain a charter that would allow them to trade in other towns without paying tolls.

The charter given on 5 May 1215 reads:

> John, by the Grace of God, etc. Know ye that we have granted and by this charter confirmed to our burgesses of Sweynesse, that they may go and come through all our land with their merchandise, to buy and sell and do business, well and in peace, freely and quietly and honourably; and that they be quit of tolls, passage, pontage, stallage and lastage and all other customs; saving in all things the liberties of our city of London. Wherefore, we will and firmly command, that our aforesaid burgesses of Sweynesse and their heirs be quit by us and our heirs for ever, throughout all our lands, buying and selling, and transacting business, as is aforesaid … Given … at Reading.

On producing a certificate, the citizens of Sweynesse were now free to trade in any town, save London, without having to pay tolls such as passage (for using a ferry-boat in or near a town), pontage (a toll for crossing a bridge in or near a town), stallage (the right to erect a stall within a town without having to pay for the privilege) and lastage (the right to peddle within a town without paying for the privilege).

Throughout May the kingdom edged closer to civil war: John had arrayed his forces in the vicinity of Windsor; the rebel barons had occupied London. The Welsh March, however, was in turmoil: Giles and his younger brother, Reginald, had taken, without a fight, all the castles that had formally belonged to their father. Gower, alone, remained loyal to the king and for that it was about to pay a heavy price. To the west, Rhys Ieuanc, lord of Cantref Mawr and Cantref Bychan, had taken the offensive, running amok in Dyfed before taking possession of Kidwelly and Carnwyllion; he was now poised to descend on Gower in support of Giles, his uncle, for Rhys's father, Gruffudd (d.1201), had married Giles's sister, Matilda (d.1210).

> Thereupon, he [Rhys Ieuanc] advanced on Gower, first taking the Castle of Loughor, after which he laid siege to the castle of Hugh de Miles [at Llandeilo Talybont] because the garrison resisted him, but he took the castle by force, putting the garrison to fire and sword. The following day he made for Sweynesse, and for fear of him the garrison burned the town, but he, not being put off by this setback, made for the Castle of Oystermouth and there encamped that night. The following day he took the Castle of Oystermouth and burned the town. And at the end of three days he took all the castles of Gower. Thus he departed joyfully victorious.

John put his name to Magna Carta on 10 June 1215, thereby temporarily averting civil war, but by the end of September his failure to honour the agreement only led to such a war. Giles soon came to terms with John 'for fear of the pope', as he had been excommunicated. Writs dated 21 October gave instructions for Giles to be restored to most of his father's English estates, and Marshal was ordered to hand over Gower. On his way home from John's court Giles was taken ill at Gloucester and died on 17 November. John responded with typical lack of tact, issuing orders for the de Breos estate to revert to the Crown, forcing Giles's brother, Reginald, to rebel and align himself with Llywelyn, who's daughter, Gwladus, he married.

During the first week of December, Llywelyn, the acknowledged leader of up to a dozen princes, marched on Carmarthen which surrendered to him after a five-day siege. Llywelyn then led the confederation of princes through Dyfed and Ceredigion, the *Brut* listing ten castles captured or destroyed before the end of the year. Sweynesse and Kidwelly are listed among them—a mistake surely as Gower belonged to Reginald and he was now Llywelyn's vassal; it is far more likely that Sweynesse and Kidwelly were added to the list because Rhys Ieuanc attacked them earlier that same year.

At Aberdyfi the princes assembled to decide what should be done with their conquests. Llywelyn wisely took nothing for himself, the conquered lands being divided by council among the brotherly princes, Maelgwn and Rhys Gryg, and their nephews, Rhys Ieuanc and Owain, helping to maintain their loyalty to Llywelyn, rather than John's overlordship.

On 20 May 1216 the rebels suffered a demoralizing defeat at Lincoln, but Reginald remained steadfastly loyal to the rebel cause. John died on 19 October 1216; his passing should have brought an end to the fighting, but the civil war continued, even though, on 28 October, John's nine-year-old son, Henry, was crowned king at Gloucester and the respected William Marshal became regent. In a bid to appease die-hard rebel barons the new government declared, on 11

November, that it would honour a slightly modified version of Magna Carta, but it was not until early June 1217 that Reginald took advantage of the safe passage he had been offered to declare his allegiance to the young king, a move that led to other rebel barons following suit.

A writ dated 23 June gave instructions for the Breos estates in Herefordshire to be handed over to Reginald. On 24 June he was granted possession of the baronies of Barnstaple and Totnes, and at the same time instructions were sent to the justiciar in Ireland for the restoration of Limerick and other Munster estates. The recovery of Bramber came later. Reginald may have come to terms with the king, but in doing so he incurred the wroth of his overlord, Llywelyn; this was to cost Reginald dearly and cause a feud between himself and the eldest son of his departed brother, William the Younger. Gower was to suffer from devastation and the evils of ethnic cleansing, so much so that a poet posed the question: 'are not the women of Sweynesse altogether widows?'.

CHAPTER V
The Misrule of the de Breoses

The *Brut* states that when Llywelyn learned that Reginald had renounced his pact
he

> laid siege to Brecon, and the burgesses … made peace with him, offering five
> hostages from amongst the most influential of their number against paying
> him 100 marks to spare the town. Llywelyn, then, made for Gower, taking a
> course over the Black Mountains, where many of his packhorses were lost, and
> encamped at Llangwig. When Reginald saw the damage that Llywelyn inflicted
> upon his Welsh possessions he took six knights with him and surrendered to
> Llywelyn. The following day he gave the castle of Sweynesse [and the lordship
> of Gower] to Llywelyn who entrusted the acquisition to Rhys Gryg. And there
> Llywelyn stayed for a few days before marching on Dyfed to fight the Flemings.

Llywelyn's alley, Rhys Gryg—Rhys the hoarse—was an aggressive, stubborn man
who, the previous year, had acquired Kidwelly, Carnwyllion and most of Cantref
Mawr and Cantref Bychan; now, with Gower added to his possessions, he was lord of
almost all that had once been granted to Hywel ap Goronwy in 1106.

Towards the close of 1217 forces in support of the new king laid siege to
Caerleon Castle, at that time in the hands of the Welsh, after which the *Brut* relates
that 'Rhys Gryg overthrew Sweynesse and all its [subsidiary] castles to the ground.
And he drove all the English from that land and took from them their chattels, as
much as he pleased, and he drove with them their wives and children without any
hope of ever returning. And he divided their lands between Welshmen'. In connection with these events the poet, Prydydd y Moch, extolled the actions of Rhys Gryg
as follows: 'And Abertawe, town of calm. Broken towers, and today is there not
peace? In Abertawe, strong key of England. Are not the women altogether widows?'.

Although the *Brut* implies that Rhys Gryg overthrew the castles of Gower in
retaliation for the Crown's attack on Caerleon, it is more likely that he rendered
them useless to prevent English settlers making use of them, should they rebel. It is
also feasible that, having annexed Gower, he encountered opposition to his rule

from the most influential English settlers. There is, however, no other evidence to support the view that the English were expelled, although there are strong indications that principal landowners were replaced by Welshmen. Reference has already been made to Hareng whom Llywelyn ousted from the fief of Penmaen, but Llywelyn also granted the dispersed manor of Landimore and the manor of Kilvey to Morgan Gam, lord of Afan, in return for the service of one fully-armed knight. In the case of Landimore this must have involved ousting a successor of the William de Turberville who had held the fief in 1166.

The one person to epitomize Welsh resurgence in Gower is Gruffydd Gwyr. Wood, in his *Rivers of Wales*, published in 1814, related: 'In the angle formed by the rivers Twrch and Tawe is Yniscedwin, anciently the patrimony, or acquisition, of Gruffydd Gwyr, the founder of a family of opulence and authority in Gower about the end of the 12th - beginning of the 13th century'. Furthermore, amongst the parochialia of Edward Lloyd (*c.*1597) is a note by one of his correspondents to the effect that Gower 'was called of one Gruffydd Gwyr who sometime possessed the same, and for that great son of Cadifor ... [who] came in company of ... who conquered that country and had part of it given him who was, therefore, called Gruffydd Gwyr of ye sundry conquests thereof, etc'.

Others sources state that Gruffydd was the third son of Cadifor, the man who had availed himself of Glyntawe and part of (northern) Gower, and that Yniscedwyn was Gruffydd's share of the patrimony. Llywelyn, in his march on Gower, must have passed through Glyntawe and it is, therefore, feasible that Gruffydd joined forces with him to be rewarded with the fief of Knelston and possibly other lands. Gruffydd is supposed to have left numerous descendants in Glamorgan and Gower who assumed various surnames—certainly many Welshmen in later centuries have claimed descent from him.

With the civil war in England almost at an end, Llywelyn did homage to the young king in March 1218, agreeing to persuade the lesser princes to do the same. Rhys Gryg, alone, remained obdurate, refusing to pay homage, or to hand over captured territory such as Gower. The uneasy peace that followed may have suited Reginald, but he now had to fight a series of legal battles with contenders who laid claim to all or part of his lands, the most important contender being his nephew, John, the first-born son of his late brother, William the Younger.

Born on 6 October 1197, John de Breos is said to have been nicknamed Tadey or Tadody, and fostered in Gower by a Welshman according to one source, by a Welshwoman by another. At the age of 13, when his father had been imprisoned at Windsor Castle, John was placed in custody until released in January 1218. John immediately began proceedings for the recovery of what should have been his father's inheritance had he lived, his mother claiming Bramber as her dower. Gower was initially left out of the reckoning as that was in the hands of Rhys Gryg.

With Reginald now in royal favour, the suit was repeatedly postponed. Suspicions were then raised as to John's loyalty when, in 1219, he married

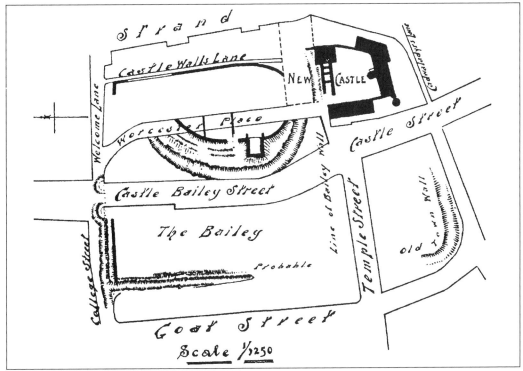

Plan of Swansea Castle as associated with John de Breos

Llywelyn's daughter, Margaret, and his mother married Rhys Gryg. On 29 September 1219 John changed his plea, claiming only Bramber, but Reginald still managed to frustrate him. Then, in 1220, John's circumstances changed in that firstly his wife gave birth to a son, and secondly he gained territory from an unexpected quarter, for in July Llywelyn entered Ystrad Tywi and skirmished with Rhys Gryg at Carmarthen bridge where he forced him to surrender all land that had been captured since 1215.

Llywelyn had been empowered to return the captured territories to their rightful owners, which he now did, though he handed over Gower to John and not Reginald as the Crown would have wished. John was becoming increasingly frustrated by his uncle's delaying tactics and, in December 1221 he obtained Llywelyn's permission to repair the ruined castle of Sweynesse. Then, encouraged by Llywelyn, John made an incursion into Brecknock, burning townships, killing Reginald's men and causing damage to the value of £600. When he stood before the king's justices in February 1222, John denied any involvement in the attack and no more is heard of the matter.

Despite the *Brut*'s statement that Sweynesse Castle was repaired, historians still ponder on whether the slighted castle was completely rebuilt in stone, for it is possible that John set in motion work that would be carried out over several years.

The remains of a stone castle were found in 1913, immediately to the north of the castle ruins that can be seen today. It appears that the old motte had been levelled and the spoil used to fill in the accompanying ditch, a new ditch being cut to enclose a larger area. About 3m inside the new ditch the remains of a 2m thick curtain wall were found, surviving in places to a height of 2m. The curtain wall would have been oval in plan, and at the south-western curve a 9m square platform was found, undoubtedly the base of a square tower and possibly the site of a draw-bridge. The interior of the new castle has not been excavated, but like Carmarthen—rebuilt at roughly the same date—it probably contained a hall, chambers, chapel, exchequer offices, bakehouse, kitchen, granary, wine cellar, armoury, stables and a well.

The area enclosed by the curtain wall may have been known as the 'inner bailey' because, by the late 13th century, another bailey makes its appearance in the records and, like the castle described above, there is no record as to when this stone walled 'outer bailey' was built. Sections of the surrounding ditch have been found at several locations, up to 3m deep, from which fragments of 13th and 14th century jugs have been retrieved. The foundations of the two drum towers which flanked the north gate were laid bare in 1845 and again in 1911. This gateway was known as Harold's Gate; another (unnamed) gateway dominated the opposing wall to the south. Several towers are referred to in later documents, including ones called Donald, Singleton and Bokynham.

The internal area of the outer bailey is believed to have been 4.3 acres, almost as large as the 5-acre interior of the Roman fort at *Leucarum*. The garrison may have been similar to the one recorded at Carmarthen in 1228—30 men-at-arms and 10 crossbowmen—of which John had custody between 1226-28. Security at the castle was the responsibility of a constable; the name of the earliest one—William Revel—is to be found in a grant dated to around 1200.

John is also associated with Parc-le-Breos—first mentioned in a confirmatory charter of about 1230 as *Silva de Bruiz*—a 2,000-acre deer park of extensive woodland centred on two narrow valleys (Green Cwm and Llethrid Cwm), the whole enclosed by a bank topped by a fence, in places reinforced by a wall and an internal ditch. The entrance to the park was near what later became known as the Park Mill, now a heritage centre. A hunting lodge probably existed at Parc-le-Breos House. After John's line had expired in the early 14th century, and Gower had become the property of non-resident lords, the park declined until it was disparked in the early 15th century, parcels of land being let to several tenant farmers.

It is reasonable to assume that, during John's rule, at least half of the subsidiary castles slighted by Rhys Gryg were repaired, though none of them, except Loughor, in stone. It is also likely that after 1220 a number of churches were rebuilt to withstand attack: narrow windows were sited high up in thick walls, roofs were flagged, heavy oak doors reinforced with criss-cross strips of iron to prevent attackers from axing their way into the nave. The most obvious feature of defence was the tower, the most impressive being the one at Llanrhidian where access was from the nave, the stairs leading to a door that gave access to a first floor room above the nave where crossbowmen could discharge their bolts through narrow windows. The stairs continued up to the battlements which were often concealed by 'hording'; that is, a projecting blockhouse, the wooden walls loopholed, providing maximum protection and excellent fields of fire. Despite later renovations, some 13 Gower churches still display features connected with defence. These strongholds first appeared in Gower probably in the late 12th century, the last to be built being Cheriton in the early 14th century.

John's lengthy suit finally came to a close early in 1226 when Reginald yielded Bramber and the manor of Tetbury in Gloucester on condition that John made no further claims to the de Breos estate. From then on, John's relationship with the Crown improved to the extent that, on 25 October 1226, he was granted custody of the then small counties of Carmarthen and Cardigan, which he held until April 1228, the year in which Reginald died.

In retrospect, John may be seen as a young man who had tried hard to recover what was rightfully his. He even appears as a generous benefactor: he gave Ilston Church to the Hospitallers, fishing rights on the Tawe to Neath Abbey, parcels of land to Talley Abbey—but from 1229 on there are hints of another side to his character, one that is evident in all the de Breoses, for there are several instances which show him to have been a grasping tyrant.

Eleven years earlier, Llywelyn had given the dispersed manor of

Llanrhidian Church Tower, once a place of refuge from Welsh attacks. The door and large windows were installed when defence was no longer required

Cheriton Church—purpose-built for defence in the early 14th century.
Note how high up the widows are in the walls

Landimore to Morgan Gam who, in turn, made it the dowry of his daughter, Maud, when she married Sir Gilbert de Turberville. Some time after 1229, when John was no longer Llywelyn's vassal, he dispossessed Sir Gilbert of the manor, which in turn led to several law-suits. Another instance concerns Parc-le-Breos as its creation may have involved appropriating land from neighbouring fiefs, even the relocation of a village and church in the fief of Penmaen.

In October 1229, Hubert de Burgh, justiciar of England, persuaded the young Henry III to grant him the counties of Carmarthen and Cardigan as Marcher lordships. A month later de Burgh was granted the homage and service of John, which meant that John was no longer Llywelyn's vassal, but de Burghs. Llywelyn felt threatened by de Burgh's rise to power, the more so when, after the death of Reginald's son, William V, he received word in May 1231 that the bulk of the de Breos estate would pass to de Burgh. In mid-June, Llywelyn fell upon Montgomery, then marched down the Wye Valley, leaving a trail of destruction as he passed through de Burgh's territory; turning west, he besieged Neath, burning both the town and castle. Gower he left untouched, though he must have marched through the lordship on his way to destroy the town and castle of Kidwelly.

John died 'a cruel death' at Bramber as a result of a riding accident on 16 July 1232, being 'drawn at his horse's tail'. His eldest son, William VI, was still a minor at the time, and for the next nine years custody of Gower passed through several hands. Within days of John's death, de Burgh lost his position as justiciar of England to a rival, Peter des Roches, bishop of Winchester, who, on 19 September 1232, gave his nephew, Peter de Rivaux, custody of much that had been de Burgh's possessions, including Gower, which he held until his uncle fell from power in March 1234.

In 1233, Henry III came into conflict with the new earl of Pembroke, William Marshall II. The dispute led to an outbreak of hostilities in South Wales and the Welsh princes wasted no time in taking advantage of the situation. The following year the incompetent Henry was persuaded to appease the various factions. The Sweynesse burgesses were granted a worthless charter (dated 8 March) which confirmed the one given to them by King John allowing then to trade in other towns without paying tolls. In May, Henry pardoned two Sweynesse bailiffs for their part in the revolt, both of whom were Welshmen.

Another rebel to be pardoned was Richard Siward, lord of Llanbleddian in Glamorgan; on 17 July 1234 he was granted custody of Gower. During his term of office the king notified him that a certain matter had been brought to his attention, to whit, a Robert de Penres had offered John's widow, Margaret, £100 for the marriage of Agnes, daughter and heiress of William de la Mere. Margaret never received payment because Siward's predecessor, Peter de Rivaux, had kept the money for himself. In consequence, Siward was instructed to redress the wrong.

As to Agnes de la Mere, the family name appears in Bishop Anselm's confirmatory charter (c.1230) to the Hospitallers, which states: 'gift of Robert de la Mere, the church of Porteynon and the mansion house near the church … and 10 acres of land in the fief of Oxwich'. It is not known when the properties were gifted (possibly in the late 12th century), but the wording of the charter suggests that Robert de la Mere held the fief of Porteynon and probably Oxwich as well. It is conceivable that, as a result of his marriage to Agnes, Robert de Penres acquired the two fiefs mentioned—they undoubtedly belonged to the Penres family in the 14th century.

Sir William de Breos VI

On his 21st birthday in 1241, William de Breos VI succeeded to his father's estate. Three years later he saw active service in West Wales. In 1252 he was involved in what may have been a border dispute with his Welsh neighbour, Rhys Fychan, a grandson of Rhys Gryg. Rhys Fychan is reputed to have burnt one of William's castles, possibly Penlle'r castell which had been built about this time (though perhaps not finished) to bar entry into Gower from the north. When Henry III heard of the trouble he ordered William to desist from further action and asked the seneschal of Carmarthen to mediate.

More serious trouble soon followed. Llywelyn ap Gruffydd, prince of Gwynedd (better known as Llywelyn the Last), had, in the space of a few years, proved himself to be at least as able as his grandfather, Llywelyn ap Iorwerth. In 1257, Llywelyn marched south, the *Annals Cambriae* reporting that he 'came to Kidwelly, Carnwyllion and Gower, where he burned all that belonged to the English in the aforesaid lands, as also in Abertawe, and having subjugated the Welshmen of those parts he returned home at Easter'.

The records are silent as to whether William was at Abertawe when the town was burnt, or whether he took part in the disastrous offensive that followed. A large force of English troops under Stephen Bauzan left Carmarthen to advance up the Tywi Valley. On 2 June they were surprised and routed at the Battle of Cymerau. Bauzan was killed in the fighting, as were 3,000 of his troops, and the remnants of his army barely made it back to Carmarthen. The southern princes followed up the victory by marching on Gower again.

When civil war broke out in England in 1263, William aligned himself with rebel barons, but soon changed sides. He remained loyal to the king, despite the fact that his English lands were plundered by rebel forces. On 4 August 1265 he fought at the Battle of Evesham, which ended the war in the king's favour. For his part in the battle, William must have felt that the king, out of gratitude, would turn a blind eye to any liberties that he might take. That William took liberties becomes apparent many years later when, in 1302, the king's attorney stated that, after Evesham, William had usurped royal jurisdiction. As a Marcher lord, William had the right, within Gower, to issue writs and try men for serious offenses, and no doubt felt aggrieved by the fact that his tenants had a right to appeal against his judgements by taking their grievances to the County Court at Carmarthen, even though the officials at Carmarthen dealt with appeals on behalf of the king. By usurping royal jurisdiction he denied his tenants the right to appeal to the king's representatives at Carmarthen; he also excused himself from attending the County Court as a juror.

At a later date it becomes apparent that the king's attorney had got the date of William's usurpation wrong, for in 1306 a jury stated that William withdrew from the jurisdiction of Carmarthen after the Battle of Cymerau in 1257, when his father-in-law, Nicholas de Moels, was seneschal of Carmarthen. They alleged that William had married Agnes, the daughter of de Moels, and was, therefore, able to usurp royal jurisdiction on account of the 'affinity and tolerance' of his father-in-law—in short, de Moels allowed him to get away with it.

In 1272, Henry was succeeded by his son, Edward I. Four years into his reign, Edward aimed to take advantage of the current bout of dissension between the Welsh princes to settle with Llywelyn once and for all. Throughout the winter of 1276-77 preparations were made for a three-pronged attack on Llywelyn and his vassals, William serving with the army which, leaving Carmarthen, advanced up the Tywi Valley. No details of the campaign are known, but on 11 April, Llywelyn's southern vassal, Rhys ap Maredudd, submitted; other princes soon followed suit. Finally, Llywelyn was forced to yield in the face of tremendous odds.

Trouble came to William from another quarter in 1278 when William Beauchamp, earl of Warwick, laid claim, in the king's court, to the castle of

Sweynesse and the lordship of Gower. Beauchamp based his claim on hereditary right, pleading that Earl William de Newburgh (whom he falsely stated to be his ancestor) had formally held both the castle and the lordship. In his defence William de Breos referred to the charter of 1203 (see pp.45-46)—to which Beauchamp countered that the charter made no mention of the castle, that the charter had been issued under duress, and that the present William de Breos had succeeded to Gower not by hereditary right, but as a result of an agreement between John and Reginald de Breos. In response, William de Breos averred that the castle was part of the lordship, that his great-grandfather had been succeeded by his grandfather, William the Younger, and that the lordship finally passed to his father, John, after he had reached maturity. The earl of Warwick contended that William the Younger had never been in possession of Gower and repeated his claim that John had acquired the lordship by agreement. The case was adjourned several times until, in 1280, a verdict was reached in de Breos's favour.

William was issued with a safe conduct in March 1282 in order to go on pilgrimage to Santiago de Compostela in Spain, though whether he ever went is unrecorded. Before his departure a revolt broke out in North Wales that quickly spread. Edward's response was to advance on the kernel of the trouble, leaving the earl of Pembroke to deal with the rebellious princes of South Wales. A force that included 700 men from Kidwelly and 360 from Gower under the command of John de Penres proceeded up the Tywi into Cardiganshire. (The Welsh Rolls record that John de Penres was appointed constable of Dynefwr and Carreg Cennen Castles during Edward's earlier campaign of 1277.) On his return in September John de Penres garrisoned Dynefwr Castle until, joined by the Kidwelly men and 70 Englishmen, he made an attack on Gruffydd ap Maredudd, whose castle he burned and destroyed. Chancery accounts record payments made to the troops who garrisoned Dynefwr during September. One entry records: 'To John de Penres, 12 men-at-arms, 12 grooms, one standard bearer and 72 foot soldiers - £1 17s. 8d.'.

Payments such as the above came from England, the silver pennies transported in barrels or sacks. Chancery accounts dated October 1282 record a shipment of 1,000 marks from Lincoln to Chepstow, the escort provided being one trooper and 6 foot soldiers. Three troopers and 12 foot soldiers escorted the shipment through Glamorgan. 400 men were requisitioned to escort the convoy past Sweynesse 'because Llywelyn and his men were on the far side of the water', meaning the River Loughor. Finally, 60 foot soldiers accompanied the shipment to Kidwelly.

Llywelyn was killed in a skirmish near Builth on 11 December, but the revolt continued into the winter of 1282-83. The sheer size of Edward's army in North Wales created tremendous logistical problems and while he was at Conway he feared that his troops might starve. The Welsh Rolls for March 1283 refer to victuals bought at Yarmouth by the merchants of Sweynesse for the use of the king in Wales.

In 1284 Edward toured Wales, staying at Kidwelly before moving on to Gower to be received by William at Oystermouth Castle on 10 and 11 December. It has been suggested that Oystermouth was chosen because Sweynesse Castle was in a state of disrepair, a suggestion based on the fact that in an inquisition of 1319 it was reported that William had sold both the north and south gates of the outer bailey and that he (or his son) had sold off two towers as well. It is, however, far more likely that William was anxious show off his relatively new stone-built castle at Oystermouth.

The oldest part of Oystermouth Castle is the central block. The late 13th century additions were, for the most part, the remains which can be seen today, the exceptions being the three-story building attached to the south-eastern corner of the central block (which includes the chapel), and those adjoining the curtain wall on the west. Even today the remains of this castle are impressive. Apart from Sweynesse and Oystermouth, there were four other castles built/rebuilt in stone during the late 13th to early 14th century—Loughor (the remains of which can be seen today), Penrice (probably built by the Robert de Penres who died in 1283), Pennard (which also belonged to William), and Weobley (which is a fortified manor house).

Some of William's tenants had migrated to Carreg Cennen in 1283, declaring that they would rather live under the king than a Marcher lord. Two years later it was the Welsh who showed their discontent, for in the autumn of 1285, William complained to the king that a number of Welshmen had left his lordship to live in Is-Cennen, then Crown property. A commission was appointed to investigate the matter, but the results of the inquiry are not known. What is known is that the

Oystermouth Castle as it may have appeared to Edward I when he stayed there in 1284

Pennard Castle, a late 13th- to early 14th-century stone castle erected over the remains of an early ring-work

Welshmen did not leave in the accepted sense—they all held land in the north-western corner of *Supraboscus,* which they and the king's agents claimed to be part of Is-Cennen. It may be that this affair led to Gower losing the land which lay between a stream called Cathan and the River Aman,[1] the same land over which, presumably, a border dispute had arisen in 1252.

Discontent with de Breos may well have been over financial matters, for, like his forebears, he seems to have been prepared to resort to all sorts of demands and illegal practices to get hold of it, including alienating his lands. He held Gower on behalf of the king, meaning he needed the king's permission to sell off property. Yet in an inquisition of 1319 it was revealed that he had alienated numerous parcels of land without the king's permission, including his demesne manor of Trewyddfa.

Another opportunity to increase his revenue came when the bishop of Llandaff (another William de Breos, reputed to be his uncle) died on 19 March 1287, William's administrators taking possession of the ecclesiastical manor of Bishopston, holding it for three years on the grounds that the lords of Gower always had custody of the manor during a vacancy of the see.[2]

In November 1290 the king's escheator objected to the seizure, claiming the manor for the Crown. William responded by saying his seneschal had seized the manor without his knowledge, then disclaimed responsibility on the grounds that his son, William VII, was in possession of the manor as lord of Gower. He also stated that he would accept any decision made by the Crown. The manor remained in the custody of the Crown until a new bishop was consecrated in 1297.

Rhys ap Maredudd, a grandson of Rhys Gryg, was the only prince of West Wales to remain loyal to Edward during the war of 1282 and was handsomely rewarded to the extent that he became lord of most of Cantref Mawr and Cantref Bychan, and also held two commotes in southern Ceredigion. Yet in spite of his loyalty he was repeatedly harassed by the justiciar of West Wales until, in 1287, he rose in revolt while Edward was on the Continent, attacking the castles of Llandovery, Dynefwr and Carreg Cennen.

On 11 June he moved his forces into Gower, to be joined by several leading Welshmen of *Supraboscus*, benefitting by their council, especially that of Einion ap Hywel. In a surprise attack on Sweynesse he burned the town, taking much spoil. He took Oystermouth Castle after a siege lasting several days, 'wasting by fire the vill and manor along with the greater part of the [English] county'. Whilst at Oystermouth 'certain of the men he captured he caused to be strangled before his very eyes', others were led away into captivity. He also 'violated the church for the sake of loot' and the wives and children who had taken refuge there he 'put to death indifferently'. Then, warned that a large force was advancing from the east, he withdrew.

It is possible that the men of *Supraboscus* rebelled against William over his demands for money. It is not known whether he had been in Gower when it was plundered, but at some point in 1287, probably after Rhys's withdrawal, he was ordered to remain in his lordship to defend it. He also had instructions to be lenient with the Gower rebels, thereby inducing them to return to the king's peace. The *Breviate of Domesday* records that Gruffydd Frych, lord of Glyntawe, Gruffydd ap Hywel, Owain Fychan, Einion ap Hywel and others, in order to obtain William's peace, offered up their woods so that they could keep their pastures and other lands. They also requested that 'the law of 12 and of inquest' (meaning trial by a 12-man jury) should take the place of judgement by an assembly of all the local landowners, though the laws themselves remained the laws of Hywel Dda. The woods that were given to William later became known as the manor of Gwaun Caegurwen.

Sir William de Breos VII

From about 1288 onwards, William appears to have left Gower in the hands of his eldest son, William (VII) the Younger, and retired to Bramber where he died on Christmas Day 1290. William the Younger had been born about 1255. At the age of about 10 he became a hostage of Simon de Montfort, leader of a reformist party of barons who died at the Battle of Evesham. He served in North Wales during the wars of 1277 and 1282, and did service with the king on the Continent in 1286. His abilities as a soldier were put to the test two years later when he took part in a campaign to quell the ongoing rebellion of Rhys ap Maredudd.

Newcastle Emlyn had been seized by the rebels and, for the purpose of recapturing the castle, William raised a force of 7 horse and 63 foot from Gower, and from elsewhere a further 3 heavy horse, 18 light horse, 2 mounted and 19 foot-crossbowmen and 400 foot soldiers. On 1 January 1288 he and his followers had blockaded Newcastle Emlyn with the aid of a volunteer force from Cardigan. The previous August an engine of war—presumably, from its description, a catapult—had been successfully used against Dryslwyn Castle, and this was now appropriated by William and taken to Newcastle Emlyn with the aid of up to 60 oxen and four wagons. A total of 480 great stones were taken from a breach at Cardigan Castle and transported by ship to Llechryd and thence by 120 packhorses to the camp at Newcastle Emlyn. Meanwhile ten Welsh 'mechanics' and 24 woodcutters prepared hurdles—portable rectangular frames reinforced with withies or wood, used to give protection to the attackers. The engine arrived at William's camp on 10 January. By the 20th the castle had fallen and William had not lost a man.

William may have proved himself an able soldier, but he had inherited debts from his father that were to dog him all his life. Even members of his own family hounded him, one being his father's third wife, Mary de Roos, who took her grievance to the king. In 1292 the king warned William that if he did not settle his outstanding debts, then his Marcher status would not prevent the king's agents from entering Gower to collect the money by distraint. There was, however, one way he could avoid being brought to book - as long as he was in the king's service he could not be sued.

An opportunity to serve the king came in the autumn of 1294 when revolts broke out throughout Wales. For his part, William joined with three other barons to raise 50 lances for service in West Wales where English settlements were being devastated. Even when the rebellion had been quelled he remained in service as 'keeper of the peace' from December 1295 till Easter the following year. Then he was off to Scotland, not alone it seems, for when the campaign had been brought to a satisfactory conclusion a safe-conduct was issued for 20 Welshmen of William de Breos to enable them to return home. By the end of 1296 he was with the king in Flanders, accompanied by a following of 200 foot soldiers.

He was still in Flanders in 1298 when the king granted him the wardship of John de Mowbray (then 12 years of age) which meant that he had custody of the Mowbray estate. The grant also gave him the right to arrange John's marriage—to his 6 or 7-year-old daughter, Alina, the couple being married in the chapel at Sweynesse Castle that same year.

In April 1298 he was appointed a commissioner of array, being instructed to raise 300 infantry from Gower and take them to Carlisle to fight the Scots. Two months later he fought at Falkirk, helping to defeat William Wallace and his Scotsmen. In connection with this campaign the chief burgess of Sweynesse was instructed to send all ships of the port, of the burthen weight of 40 tons of wine and upwards, to the king at Winchelsea for transporting troops and supplies to Scotland.

The bishop of Llandaff complained, in 1299, that William had trespassed in his manors of Bishopston and Murton, carrying off goods, imprisoning some of his men and forcing others to do suit at Sweynesse. The complaint went to court, but became mixed up in other actions against William. The fact that no mention was made of the issue in the inquest of 1306 suggests that it was eventually settled in the bishop's favour.

Prior to Lent 1300 certain tenants complained at the County Court of Carmarthen that William and his seneschal, John Iweyn (Owyn), had oppressed them. William was summoned to Carmarthen, under pain of outlawry, where he acknowledged that he owed suit there, which effectively put an end to his usurpation of royal jurisdiction. In January 1301 he appeared before the king to hear Walter de Pederton, seneschal of Carmarthen, state that Gower was part of the county of Carmarthen, that his predecessors and his tenants had always been within the jurisdiction of Carmarthen. William argued that, from the time of King John's charter, he and his ancestors had enjoyed royal jurisdiction until Pederton's summons—to which Pederton countered that the charter only conferred land to be held by knight's service, that it made no mention of royal jurisdiction. The matter was referred to the next parliament and William was ordered, under pain of forfeiture, not to injure his tenants in any way.

At the parliament of July 1302 it was revealed that, contrary to the king's mandate, William had injured certain tenants, one of whom, Sir William de Langton of Kilvrough, alleged that William's seneschal had taken him to Oystermouth and detained him until he had signed a release of all actions against de Breos. The majority of the council decided that the king should give judgement against de Breos, but none was given due the king 'wishing to deal gently' with William. Two inquiries followed, both of them annulled because they had taken place while William had been serving in Scotland.

The king showed his appreciation of William when, after the fall of Stirling Castle in July 1304, he invited certain barons to state their reward for services rendered. William requested the fullest powers of a Marcher lord be given in respect of Gower, and Edward duly granted him a charter, dated 16 October 1304, which stated that William held Gower 'of the king and his heirs' and that he had 'all manner of royal jurisdiction'.

At the parliament of March 1305, however, it was pointed out that the new charter had been issued after the king had given all Crown properties in Wales to his son, Edward, the first heir to the English throne to hold the title 'Prince of Wales'. The issue was adjourned until the next parliament to allow the king time to deliberate; until then William was to abide by the king's repeated instructions that he should not injure his tenants in any way.

Several occurrences in the months that followed were to cost William the king's favour, the most significant of which took place in the Exchequer Court where the king's justice, Roger de Hegham, having heard the plea of Mary de Roos that William still had not settled an outstanding debt of 800 marks, had no sooner pronounced judgement to the exchequer than William 'climbed onto the bar and, with grave and bitter words, found fault with the judgement'; he also hurled insults at Roger as he left the court. When told, the king gave orders for William to proceed bare-headed and unattired through the streets of London, after which William was committed to the Tower during the king's pleasure.

William incurred the king's displeasure again in the parliament of September 1305, for it was alleged that he had again injured his tenants; moreover, it was reported that he had installed a sheriff in Gower, contrary to local law and custom. The king ordered a new inquiry, one in which three judges were empowered to deal with the issues of misgovernance in Gower according to the laws and customs of those parts; they were to pursue the matter to its conclusion unless William came to terms with his tenants. The inquest was held at Sweynesse, opening on the morning of 21 February 1306. However, the main petitioners—William de Langton, Robert de Penres and others—were not present, presumably because William de Breos had settled with them out of court.

Also out of court, it would appear, the judges must have impressed upon William that if he wished to enjoy the royal jurisdiction which the king had granted him in 1304, then he would have to issue two charters—one to the burgesses of Sweynesse and one to the English and Welsh tenants of the English county of Gower.

Two charters were issued on 24 February 1306, three days after the inquiry had opened. In both charters William stated that 'we do remit all rancour ... to all ... who lately commenced suit against us' (meaning himself and his officers). Many clauses in the charter to the burgesses of Sweynesse are similar to those in the charter of Earl William, except that they are redefined in respect of changed circumstances. For instance, the charter is addressed to all burgesses 'inhabiting an entire burgage', and also those inhabiting a 'portion of a burgage'. The burgesses still had the right to take wood, except that, in the interest of conservation, it had to be 'dead wood' for their fires and only taken by day 'by the view and delivery of our forester'. They could still take oak for their houses and their ships, only now they were limited to 'four great ships' each year, although they could 'build as many [small] boats as they will, able to carry 20 casks of wine or less', paying for every new vessel 12d.

Other clauses are a clear indication of the oppression suffered at the hands of William and his seneschal. The chancery would henceforth always be kept in Gower, open to all who required writs 'without denial or difficulty' for a sum not exceeding 7d; William also vowed not to 'sell justice, nor deny it to any man'. No burgesses were to be 'carried off' as had happened to William de Langton, and none were to 'be imprisoned so long as they can find sufficient security to answer in our hundred [court], except' when they were charged with serious offences such as murder. Burgesses could only 'be amerced by the judgement and discretion of their peers'. They could not be indicted by Welshmen, nor by any of William's household, for offences committed within the borough; nor could they be seized by an 'outside' bailiff within the borough.

The charter gives insight into how the borough was administered. Each year the burgesses elected two of their number, presenting them to the seneschal who chose one of them to be the portreeve (the mayor of later times). There is no mention of a merchant guild, although they existed in most medieval boroughs; members of guilds were expected to 'pay scot and lot'; that is, contribute to the upkeep of the borough. In Sweynesse, burgesses were expected to pay 'scotage and tallage [presumed to be alternative terms for scot and lot]', but it seems that William had been in the habit of making new burgesses who were exempt from contributing to the borough funds, for in his charter William declared that 'if we shall make any new burgess', the man 'shall pay scotage and tallage ... along with the same my burgesses'. Any tolls, tallages (taxes) or aids (loans to the lords of Gower) were to 'be assessed and levied by the burgesses'. No 'outside' merchant was allowed to trade within the borough, or in Gower, except the burgesses of Loughor.

There are several references to domestics, to cattle and goods, and to men residing in the borough 'who shall not be burgesses', who were known as *chensers* and who paid 4d a year to live and practice a trade within the borough. There is also a reference to a ferry which, in later times, crossed the river in the area now occupied by Sainsbury's supermarket. One grievance concerned freedom to travel, for William made a commitment that the burgesses 'may have the king's highway and all their accustomed roads, open and free ... without ... hindrance from any man'.

The charter mentions a tax on wine, a commodity that seems to have been shipped into the town in considerable quantities; it also states that the burgesses may 'have pit coal in *Byllywasta*[3] without hindrance ... to supply all their necessities', but they were not permitted to sell it to strangers. A document produced 19 years later mentions 'mines of sea coal near la Clun' (Clyne). Less than 50 years later it becomes apparent that the most productive coal mine in Wales was at Llansamlet, near the River Tawe. Coal from both locations was undoubtedly shipped to ports such as Bristol.

Another grievance was that the burgesses and their domestics had been compelled 'to go beyond the limits of Gower' when part of a military force. They were henceforth only to be employed 'within the limits of Gower ... as is contained in their original charter'. The most unusual thing about William's charter is that he bound himself and his heirs to pay 500 marks to the king, and 500 marks to the burgesses, should the terms of his charter be violated; this is a sure indication of how much pressure had been put on him by the three judges—he certainly did not grant the charter out of the goodness of his heart.

The charter addressed to the men of the English county of Gower, both English and Welsh, contains material that relates mainly to the administration of justice. Several clauses establish that all judgement should be at the discretion and arbitration of the suitors who, in most cases, were the lords of the 12 'old knights' fiefs'.

Weobley Castle, a fortified manor house built shortly after 1304 by David de la Bere.
It suffered damage between 1404 and 1405 at the hands of Owain Glyn Dwr's forces

A large number of land grants have survived from the period *c.*1290-1320, most of them preserved among the *Penrice and Margam Abbey mss.* The one name that appears most frequently in these manuscripts is that of Sir Robert de Penres who died *c.*1336 and who was lord of Penrice, Oxwich and Port Eynon, and who also held numerous smaller holdings throughout the peninsula. He was one of the leading petitioners in the dispute with de Breos, was several times appointed a commissioner of array on behalf of Edward ll, and in 1319 he had charge of Haverfordwest Castle in West Wales. Prior to 1300 he appears to have sub-enfeoffed William of St. Ishmaels in the fief of Horton which, until then, had been part of his fief of Penrice.

Another prominent landowner to oppose de Breos was David de la Bere. He became a mense lord in 1304 when John de Turberville, then lord of Landimore, granted him land, thereby creating the fief of Weobley, which discredits de Breos's claim that Weobley was an 'old knights' fief'. David is credited with building Weobley Castle (except for the keep), the ruins of which can be seen to today.

Some fiefs, for reasons unknown, are not listed in the charter of 1306—fiefs such as Kilvrough, belonging to William de Langton. The records do show, however, that certain families—the Penreses, the de la Meres of Llangenydd, the Scurlages of Scurlage Castle, the Mansels and the Penbrugges—dominated the affairs of late 13th- and 14th-century Gower. Members of these families were also burgesses and for good reason: rearing sheep and selling wool to seafaring merchants was profitable. In 1370-71 the mayor of London complained that wool belonging to William

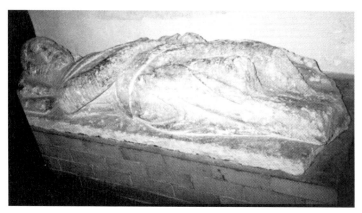

Effigy of a de le Mere in chain mail, a hand resting upon a sword hilt (c.1280), in Llangenydd Church. The legs have been broken off

Strete, valued at £254, had been seized by Richard Scurlage, Robert Penbrugge and others. The mayor demanded restoration, threatening reprisals on the Sweynesse burgesses for non-compliance.

In December 1307, Edward II (who had succeeded his father earlier that year) issued orders for the arrest of all Knights Templars and, on 7 January 1308, the sheriff of Carmarthen, accompanied by 12 horsemen, rode into Gower to take possession of the Templars' manor of Llanmadog. By September that same year a report was compiled which reveals that the manor had been quite small, little more than 115 acres, of which 52 acres were demesne, worked by 11 husbandmen who held 60 acres between them, and by four cottars. The report also mentions four men in advowry, presumably men who had taken sanctuary there. The pope suppressed the order in 1312 and Llanmadog was transferred to the Hospitallers.

Whilst William appears to have honoured the terms of his charter in the years leading up to 1314, his pigheadedness may have invited trouble from near neighbours, for in 1309 the men of Kidwelly and Is-cennen, prompted no doubt by their respective lords, Henry of Lancaster and John Giffard, entered Gower, causing much damage. It required the intervention of the justiciar of West Wales to put an end to the hostilities. Amazingly, William does not appear to have aggrieved the men of *Wallicana*, which suggests that he did not encroach upon their liberties, preferring to make use of them whenever the king called upon him to provide foot soldiers for Scotland, as in 1310, and again in 1314 when he fought at Bannockburn.

Early in 1315 the bishop of Llandaff complained before parliament that the previous year William had trespassed in the manors of Bishopston and Murton, forcing his tenants to do suit (present themselves as witnesses) at the English county court. The king ordered William to desist from oppressing the tenants and to give satisfaction to the bishop—but the bishop was not the only one to have a grievance.

Among the *Penrice and Margam Abbey mss* there are four grants, all dated to the early part of 1315, which record the sale of parcels of land in north Gower by 'William de Breos, lord of Landimore, son and heir of Sir William de Breos, lord of

Gower, to Sir Robert de Penres'—evidence that by 1315 Sir William had ousted the Turbervilles from Landimore and installed his only son, William VIII, in the manor.

In the spring of 1316, William obtained a royal licence to settle all but one of his English manors on his daughter, Alina, and her husband, John de Mowbray, who held extensive estates in the north of England. Gower was not included in these arrangements, presumably because William's intention was that it should pass to his son, William VIII, although he seems to have died between 1317 and 1319. On 24 April 1317, William married his second wife, Elizabeth de Sully, a sole heiress who brought him several manors, but gave him no children.

Atlantic storms pounded the Gower coastline in the early 14th century, besanding certain areas to the extent that the villages of Lesser Rhosili (on the platform below and to the west of Rhosili Down}, Penmaen and Pennard were eventually abandoned. The besanding at Pennard had already done sufficient damage by 1317 for William to grant a charter, dated 17 June, to his huntsman, William le Hunt, which gave him 'full liberty to hunt and take all manner of venison, foxes, hares and rabbits in the lord's rabbit warren … in the sand burrows' with full power to sell his merchandize throughout Gower. Hunts Bay, to the west of Pwlldu Head, is a reminder that William le Hunt held property in the area.

Later in 1317, William was ordered to provide 100 foot soldiers for yet another Scottish campaign.

In November that same year, at William's request, the burgesses of Sweynesse obtained a royal charter of murage and pavage, which gave them the right, for a period of 10 years, to levy a special toll on all goods entering the town for the purpose of building or repairing the town's defences, and also for paving the streets. This is not the first time the burgesses had been given such a grant, for murage is mentioned in one of the charters of 1306; they also obtained a murage and pavage grant in 1338, this time for a period of five years. On the east the town wall probably ran along the west side of the Strand, at the foot of the low ridge on which the castle stood. Turning west, the wall ran from the Strand to follow a line just south of King's Lane and King's Street (see map on p.110) where a V-shaped ditch was discovered, one that had cut into an earlier ditch; from there the wall probably ran southwards in line with Orchard Street; from a point near the Kingsway Roundabout it was joined by a stream called the Town Ditch. Both wall and Town Ditch continued southwards to enclose St. Mary's churchyard. In the 1970s, excavation for town improvements in the area between St. Mary's churchyard wall and what used to be C & A revealed a ditch, 3m deep and 10m wide, similar to the one that surrounded the castle. A little to the west of the churchyard wall the remains of a stout wall, nearly 2m thick, were found, made of sandstone and lime mortar. At one point a drainage outlet was discovered in the wall. Excavation in the late 1970s showed that a section of crenellation had collapsed into the ditch. At a point near St. David's Catholic Church the Town Ditch merged with another stream called the Cadle, which flowed eastwards from the Burrows (the low-lying area west of the town); from there the merged streams formed a wide stretch of waterway called the Pill, which flowed eastwards, past the bottom of Wind Street, to empty into the Tawe River a little to the south of Toys R Us. The town wall, which followed the Pill, then turned north up the Strand as stated above. There were several gateways in the town wall—the North Gate at the junction of Kings Lane and Kings Street, the West Gate near the Kingsway roundabout, Wassail Gate in the vicinity of Henry Hussey's statue, and the South Gate at the bottom of Wind Street. There may also have been two eastern gates, one at the bottom of Welcome Lane, one at the bottom of Castle Lane.

It is fairly certain that these defences were the result of money raised from murage, but primitive defences must have existed as far back as the early 12th century. The town's defences were maintained until the mid-17th century, after which the ditch was either filled in, or allowed to silt up; some of the gates are known to have survived well into the 18th century.

Edward II's favourite, Hugh Despenser, became lord of Glamorgan in November 1317. He was a man bent on aggrandizement, and in August 1318 the king had to issue orders for both Despenser and William to stop fighting each other. By then, William's only son was probably dead and, according to the rules of inheritance, William's son-in-law, John de Mowbray, could expect to succeed to the whole of William's estate, including Gower, but Mowbray distrusted his father-in-law, and took the precaution of making a contract with him that guaranteed his succession to Gower as, indeed, an earlier arrangement had already established his right to succeed to most of William's English estates.

Meanwhile, William arranged to sell the reversion of Gower to Humphrey de Bohun, earl of Hereford, which meant that should Mowbray and Alina die childless, then Gower would pass to the earl. William made similar arrangements to sell the reversion of Gower to two other Marcher lords. Then William went one step further, arranging to sell Gower outright to Hugh Despenser, but Hugh got wind of the extent of William's duplicity, for not only had William arranged to sell the reversion of Gower to three different lords and sell it outright, but he had also been selling off parcels of demesne land within the lordship.

William, according to the chronicler, Thomas Walsingham, was a thriftless man who wasted away his inheritance by his extravagance. He was certainly always in debt, always ready to replenish his coffer by whatever means were necessary. As William held Gower of the king he needed the king's sanction to alienate, by gift or sale, any demesne land within the lordship that would result in impoverishing his estate.

The king, prompted no doubt by Despenser, ordered an inquiry to ascertain what lands and tenements William had alienated without a royal licence. In October a jury met 'at Crymlyn in the March of Gower'; they were to discover that William and his father before him had made numerous such alienations, yet later evidence suggests that no action was taken to nullify them.

Despite William's multiple arrangements, the sale of Gower to Despenser must have been in hand by the autumn of 1319, for in a letter to his sheriff, dated 21 September, Despenser makes it plain that he was confident the business with de Breos would soon be concluded. Unfortunately for him, John de Mowbray seized the initiative, taking possession of Gower on the strength of his contract with his father-in-law. In response, Despenser persuaded the king to seize Gower on the grounds that Mowbray had taken possession of the lordship without obtaining a royal licence, but there were delays until, on 26 October 1320, the king's sub-escheator, Richard de Foxcote, was ordered to take possession. Foxcote failed to reach the Tawe, for as he approached the chapel of St. Thomas he met with 'a great multitude of Welshmen, unknown to him and armed' who compelled him to turn back. Orders were then issued for the king's escheator, Richard de Rodney, to enter the lordship. Aided by forces provided by the justiciar of Wales and by Despenser he met with no opposition and early in 1321 fines were imposed on all who had previously resisted the king's agent.

The seizure of Gower led to discontent among the Marcher lords of South Wales, many of whom loathed Despenser and so were prepared to support Mowbray's claim to Gower. Despenser put his castles in a state of readiness against invasion by a coalition of Marcher barons under the earl of Hereford. Fighting broke out on 4 May, the invaders quickly overrunning Glamorgan, capturing many of its castles. By the end of the month Despenser had no recourse but to place his remaining castles in the hands of the king.

Mowbray recovered Gower, though not without meeting some opposition, for the constable of Sweynesse Castle refused to join the rebels and had to be taken prisoner. Neath Castle also fell to the insurgents, its custodian, John Iweyn (by then in the service of Despenser) was taken as a prisoner to Sweynesse where he was executed on 28 May. The fighting, when it spread to England, took the king by surprise. On 20 August he was obliged to pardon Mowbray, allowing him to retain Gower. Two months later the king began a counter-offensive against the erstwhile rebel barons, whom he rightly judged to be without effective leadership. On 30 November he gave orders for one of his Welsh adherents, Rhys ap Gruffydd, to attack rebel strongholds in West Wales, Gower included, which he did with an army of 40 men-at-arms and 3,000 foot soldiers. By February 1322 Gower was again in the king's hands; that same month Sir Robert de Penres was commissioned to raise 400 men from Gower in support of the Crown.

The barons in England were finally defeated at Boroughbridge in Yorkshire on 16 March 1322, Mowbray being captured in the rout. After his trial he was hanged and his body, according to one source, remained suspended in chains for three years. Alina, his wife, and their son, John, were imprisoned in the Tower of London until they were transferred to the custody of Despenser's father who, 'by grave threats and fear of death', compelled Alina to surrender the reversion of Bramber to him.

Despenser the Younger soon recovered his lost possessions and wasted no time in laying claim to the forfeited lands of rebel barons; Gower was in his possession by early June. He even laid claim to the lands of his widowed sister-in-law, Lady Elizabeth de Burgh, who was kept imprisoned until, on 11 June, she agreed to exchange her lordships of Caerleon, Usk and Trellock for Gower. Before the exchange took place, Despenser ordered his sheriff of Glamorgan to plunder Gower.

Despenser often used fraud and violence to achieve his aims, although his actions were always cloaked in legalities. Nothing epitomizes this more than the way he now reclaimed Glower. In 1324 he persuaded de Breos who, according to his daughter, may have been well on the way to becoming senile, to bring an action against Elizabeth de Burgh for the recovery of what William called the '2 commotes of Uwch-coed and Is-coed which contained the whole of Gower'. William had no sooner won his case than he passed Gower on to Despenser's father who, in turn, passed it on to his son.

In 1326 a survey was carried out on all lands and rents of the bishop of St. Davids, the findings entered in what is known as the *Black Book of St. Davids*[7]. The survey states that the bishop had two manors in Gower, one in the Englishry and one in the Welshry. In the manor of Llandewi in the Englishry the bishop had 124 acres of demesne. More than 2 acres were used for cultivating fruit. A large proportion of acreage provided wheat, barley, beans, great and small oats. What acreage remained provided pasture for, amongst other things, the bishop's 8 oxen and 120 sheep. All the tenants of the manor bore English names; three of them were *coloni*, holding between a half and 2 acres, for which they paid rent and were obliged to carry out certain services such as reaping and ploughing on the bishop's land, and do suit at the bishop's court.

The manor of Llangyfelach in *Supraboscus* was huge by comparison, over 3,000 acres in extent, only 26 acres of which were demesne, worked by unfree Welsh tenants; the only crop grown here was oats. There were also an unspecified number of free Welshmen residing in the manor, holding land not as individuals, but as kindred groups known as *gwelyau*—meaning 'beds' or 'resting places'. There were seven *gwelyau* in all, each *gwely* being referred to by the name of a common ancestor, though whether the land held by each kindred group extended beyond the bounds of the manor is not known.

A good example of a *gwely* is provided by a document of 1314, which refers to land in *Supraboscus* that was occupied the sons of Owain, Caradog and Hywel Fychan. The land was referred to as Traean Meibion Meurig—meaning 'the third part of the sons of Meurig', Meurig being the common ancestor, the father of the three men mentioned above. Other early 14th-century documents relating to Landimore suggests that *gwelyau* still existed there at that time, although some free Welshmen had opted to hold their land under English tenure; that is, when a man died his lands passed undivided to just one son, usually the eldest. Until fairly recently it was possible to identify a *gwely*-like arrangement of farms at Cilibion, Dunvant and Three Crosses.

In April 1326, William de Breos died after a period of ill-health. An inquisition post mortem recorded that, at the time of his death, only a few manors remained in his possession.

By the autumn of 1326 there was a great deal of resentment towards Despenser, for not only had he become master of almost the whole of South Wales, but from 1322 onwards he had virtually ruled England on behalf of Edward II. It only took a landing in Suffolk by the king's estranged wife and 700 mercenaries for Despenser's government to collapse. Both Edward and Despenser fled to South Wales where, on 5 November, they took shelter at Neath Abbey. That same day, Edward commissioned Sir Robert de Penres and others to raise the forces of Gower to protect him. The following day, John de Langton was appointed seneschal of Gower and authorized to see to the defence of Sweynesse and to provision the town with victuals and munitions. On 10 November, Edward dispatched all his chancery papers and impedimenta to Sweynesse Castle, appointing de Langton to take charge of the escort. Whatever his intention, Edward was captured on or about 16 November, at Neath according to some sources, at Llantrisant according to others. A few days later Despenser was executed whereas Edward, after being forced to abdicate, was eventually murdered; on 25 January 1327 he was succeeded by his son, Edward III.

The new king restored Alina de Breos to Gower in March 1327, but within two weeks had to commission an inquiry into a complaint by one of her tenants, John de Mareschal, that he had been robbed, beaten and imprisoned at Swansea and Oystermouth by persons who were, presumably, acting on Alina's instructions. Early the following year Alina married Sir Richard de Peshale. Their tenure proved unpopular, although evidence of their misrule does not come to light until, on 26 January 1331, the king ordered an investigation into the complaint of Richard de Turberville that his claim to Landimore had been rejected in the County Court of Gower. Two days later the king had to appoint another commission to look into the alleged acts of oppression by Peshale and Alina that were contrary to the charter of 1306. The commission reported on the couple's failure to redress their tenants' grievances, and Gower was taken back into the king's hands. In July 1331, Alina died and there is a tradition that she was buried in St. Mary's Church, Sweynesse, her death marking the end of de Breos rule. Her tenants may have been glad to see he go, but they were not entirely impoverished as a result of her, or her father's administration, for they appear to have acquired Edward II's impedimenta. On 18 July the king commissioned de Peshale to inquire into the whereabouts of this, which included gold and silver plates, coins and jewellery, arms and armour, horses and fine raiments, all of which had gone missing. It would appear that at an unspecified date the men of Gower, both English and Welsh, the burgesses of Sweynesse and the men of Kidwelly and Carwyllion had all had a hand in misappropriating the impedimenta. Among those implicated were Sir Robert de Penres and other prominent landowners, even a rector. Goods to the value of £3,000 were recovered, but 10 years later another inquiry failed to locate what was still missing—goods estimated to be worth an incredible £60,000.

CHAPTER VI
The End of Marcher Rule

In 1327, John Mowbray II, son of Alina by her first husband, John Mowbray I, had been granted seisin of the huge Mowbray estates in the north of England even before he became of age. He still had not reached maturity when he succeeded to Gower in 1331. Chroniclers have praised him for his military prowess and his generosity, whilst royal documents record the frequency with which the king summoned him for service in Scotland and in France. These summons were almost always accompanied by the requirement that he raised troops from Gower—but John was a non-resident lord, his infrequent visits to the lordship being brief.

Nevertheless, his tenure of Gower is marked by several important occurrences, the first in 1332 when, on 31 March, the king gave permission for Bishop Henry de Gower of St. Davids to found the Hospital of the Blessed St. David in Sweynesse. The hospital was in fact an almshouse for 'priests, blind, decrepit or infirm and also other religious men in the bishopric'. It was administered by six chaplains and endowed with lands, tenements and part of the tithes of the church of the Blessed 'Marie' of Sweynesse, This is not the earliest reference to St. Mary's Church, for it appears in the valuation of church property known as the Pope Nicholas Taxation of 1291; it is also alluded to in the charter of 1306 when William VII granted that the burgesses 'be free from keeping [watch] of such as shall fly to the church [for sanctuary]; nor shall they ... be in any way liable for the escape of such persons'. After the Dissolution the hospital became an inn known as the Cross Keys which, in the 1960s, was rebuilt in a style that is redolent of the past—not a true representation perhaps, but part of the original 14th-century building can still be seen in the north wing.

Bishop Gower is also associated with the building of the new castle at Sweynesse, which is really a fortified palace. This association stems from the comments made by John Leland, historiographer of Henry VIII, in his *Itinerary in Wales*, that 'the old castle ... stood by the bishop of St. David's castle'. The new castle certainly stood near the old, immediately to the south, separated one from the other by a ditch, and within the south-eastern corner of the outer bailey. The fact

The Cross Keys Inn, formerly the site of an almshouse known as the
Hospital of the Blessed St. David, founded in 1332

that numerous interments have been found within the new castle's walls indicated that the site had once been a cemetery and may, therefore, have been linked with St. Mary's Church, but the *Black Book of St. Davids*, compiled in 1326, makes no mention of any church property at Sweynesse, nor was the new castle listed among the seven principle residences which the bishop ordered to be repaired in 1342. There is, however, one piece of evidence that has often been quoted in support of the view that the new castle had originally belonged to the Church; that is, in 1399, Bishop Guy de Mone ordained clerics at the castle chapel, but that in itself is not proof of ownership.

The remains of the new castle comprises two blocks. The southern block has three levels—a basement, a ground floor with five service rooms, and a first floor with a banqueting hall, a solar (private quarters of the lord) and two more service rooms, one above the other. A garderobe tower occupies the south-eastern corner of the block. Above the first floor is the castle's crowning glory—an arcade of pointed arches below an embattled parapet.

The arches serve no military purpose and resemble those at the bishop's palaces at St. Davids and Lamphey in Pembrokeshire, both of which were built during the early part of the bishop's episcopate. It is the presence of these arcades that give support to the belief that the new castle had been built by Bishop Gower.

The origin of the arcades, however, can be better explained as the workmanship of itinerant craftsmen who built the hospital and who had previously worked on the bishop's palaces in Pembrokeshire. The same craftsmen must surely have been commissioned to construct the arcading at Sweynesse; they may even have been responsible for building the new castle—but for whom?

Tradition attributes the new castle to John Mowbray II, despite the fact that he already had a serviceable castle in the town. There is, however, the view that the new castle was the work of the spendthrift William de Breos VII, a lord who, unlike Mowbray, would have resided in Gower on numerous occasions. If this were so, then the arcading (which has the undeniable appearance of a later addition) would have been added sometime after 1332.

The north-east block of the new castle has been described as both a keep and a tower. It is almost square in plan, measuring 12.4m by 11m externally. Little remains of its original construction—the first floor and most of the south and west walls were rebuilt in the early 19th century when the tower was converted for use as

*Swansea Castle showing its crowning glory—
an arcade of pointed arches below its embattled parapet*

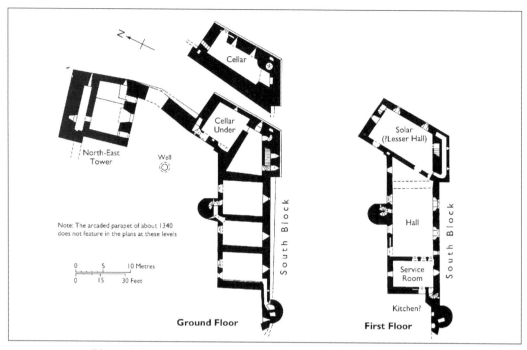

Z

Cellar

Cellar
Under

North-East
Tower

Well

Note: The arcaded parapet of about 1340
does not feature in the plans at these levels

0   5   10 Metres
0   15   30 Feet

South Block

Ground Floor

Solar
(?Lesser Hall)

Hall

Service
Room

Kitchen?

South Block

First Floor

Plan of the surviving remains of Swansea Castle, built c.1300,
probably by the spendthrift William de Breos VII

a debtor's prison. The curtain wall that connected the tower to the south block has also been extensively rebuilt even though it is now ruinous. What remained of the north curtain wall was demolished in 1912, but a photograph taken at that time shows that a passageway ran through the length of the wall as first floor level; above

The Debtors' Prison at the castle

80

this there had been a wall walk with an inner and outer parapet. The castle gateway could only have been on the west, flanked no doubt by drum towers, of which nothing remains. A well, 12m deep, existed in the eastern part of the courtyard, the present surface of which is now 1m above the original courtyard floor.

Mowbray seems to have been a man with a conciliatory nature, and his concordant rule must have lent itself to the prosperity of the town. A fragment of a jug found at the Cross Keys Inn points to imports from Rouen. Other shards found in the Medieval layers of the town point to trade with Bristol from whence came various types of glazed pottery. Ships were bigger, too, for an indenture made at Sweynesse on 11 August 1335 records a payment of £10 to two burgesses, Robert de Weston and Piers de la Bere, masters of the *Nicholas* and the *Blithe* respectively, for their ships to be prepared for war with double crews for service with the king's admiral. The *Nicholas* had a capacity of 100 tons of wine, the *Blithe* 60 tons.

But trouble was never far away, for the northern border of the lordship had still not been established by 1334 because, in that year, marauders from Is-cennen plundered the men of *Supraboscus*, though not without suffering loss. The following year the men of Gower returned the visit, killing nine Is-cennen men and capturing others whom they imprisoned at Sweynesse.

The Black Death must have swept through Gower in 1349-50, depopulating the lowland areas by as much as 50%, disrupting trade and causing serious labour shortages. Yet, locally, the records are silent about this event as, indeed, they are about the recurrences in 1361 and 1369.

The Penreses had their troubles too, for sometime after the death of Sir Robert de Penres part of the family estate became the property of an intruder, Sir Rhys ap Gruffydd, the same who had been active in Gower in 1321 on behalf of Edward II. The evidence comes from an inquisition post-mortem into the estate of Sir Rhys which shows that, at the time of his death in 1356, he held the manors of Penrice, and Port Eynon (and also the manor of Caergurwen—the woods surrendered to William de Breos VI in 1287). Regrettably, no satisfactory explanation can be given for Sir Rhys's intrusion into Penrice and Port Eynon; suffice to say that both manors were again in the hands of the Penres family by 1400.

The Beauchamps
In the early 1350s, Thomas Beauchamp I, earl of Warwick (grandson of the William Beauchamp who had unsuccessfully laid claim to Gower in 1278), brought a suit for the recovery of the lordship. In June 1354 he won his case on the grounds that William de Breos VII's gift of the lordship to his daughter, Alina, had been illegal and that John Mowbray I's tenure had come about by force of arms (1319).

One of the pleas of this suit, dated 1353, lists 24 fiefs in Gower at that time, although even this figure falls short of the true total. The plea states that there were seven castles held by the holders of fiefs—Penrice, Oxwich, Port Eynon (which may have stood at Salthouse), Landimore, Leyshanston (probably Weobley), Loughor and Talybont. There were also three castles in the lord's possession—Sweynesse, Oystermouth and Pennard.

Within a year of making good his title to Gower, Earl Beauchamp found himself involved in a lengthy litigation with Thomas de Avene (whose father was lord of Aberafan and Sully) over the manor of Kilvey, and also with Sir Richard de Turberville over the manor of Landimore. Both Thomas and Sir Richard took their grievances to the County Court of Carmarthen, claiming they held their respective manors of the prince of Wales (the Black Prince) by deed of Llywelyn ap Iorwerth. This suit led to the revival of the old argument of whether Gower was subject to Carmarthen. The outcome was that Earl Beauchamp not only lost his case against de Avene and de Turberville, but that he temporarily lost his Marcher status.

Earl Beauchamp was, nevertheless, one of the king's leading war lords, so it is hardly surprising that, by a royal charter dated 14 July 1360, he regained the latter. Like his predecessors he was often called upon to provide troops, one instance being stated in the Close Rolls for 19 September 1356 when he was ordered to raise 40 of his best Welsh archers from Gower and send them to Liverpool at the king's wages.

In spite of its small size, its location and the probability that it had suffered a visitation by the Black Death in 1361, Gower was undoubtedly one of Beauchamp's most profitable holdings; this is confirmed by the receiver's account for the year ending Michaelmas (29 September) 1367. The account is remarkable in that not only is it the earliest financial record of the lordship to survive, but it shows that Beauchamp received over £600 from Gower, £193 6s. 8d of which came from the perquisites of his courts. With regards to Sweynesse, the account makes it plain that the collection of dues was in the hands of the burgesses, the portreeve handing over the money, along with the borough accounts, to the earl's receiver who prepared the account for the lordship. The account mentions that three fairs were held in the borough each year—on 11 November, 7 July and 15 August.

Thomas Beauchamp I died in 1369 to be succeeded by his second son, Thomas ll. There is evidence that, by the time of Thomas II's tenure, the outer bailey of Sweynesse Castle was occupied by burgages, some of which where held by prominent landowners such as John de Penres and Sir John de la Bere. It is possible that, originally, the outer bailey had been designed to accommodate those who were obliged to do castle guard at Sweynesse, but by 1324 this may no longer have been the case, for in that year a John Pistor had disposed of a piece of land in the bailey. It appears the 'knights' may have converted their holdings into burgages or sold them to burgesses who were not obliged to perform castle guard. By the late 14th century even the gates and towers of the outer bailey had been sold off by the de Breoses.

Several burgages within the outer bailey at Sweynesse were subject to leases in 1383. One states that John de Penres, grandson of Sir Robert de Penres, granted to John de Horton 'a place burgage lying in the castle bailey between the garden of John de Horton on the west, the common road on the east, the land against the bailey wall on the north, and the tenement of the said John on the south'. This gave

John de Horton a compact holding in the bailey which, many years later, became occupied by one of Sweynesse's most impressive buildings, the Plas (the Place), home to many notable figures who became seneschals of Gower.

In 1387, Thomas Beauchamp II was one of several who offended King Richard II. The king bided his time. Then, in June 1396, the king appears to have encouraged Thomas Mowbray, earl of Norfolk, to bring a suit for the recovery of Gower, which Mowbray did, claiming that his grandfather, John de Mowbray II, had been dispossessed of Gower in 1354 by a verdict that had been given in error. The proceedings were discontinued because Thomas Beauchamp II, knowing the king to be against him, conceded Gower to Mowbray.

Gower must have been a grievous loss to Beauchamp, but he soon learned that the king intended to destroy him financially. On 1 June 1397 he was ordered to reimburse Mowbray with all the profits he had received from Gower since 1383—a staggering £5,337 6s. 8d. which could only be paid by installments. Further humiliation came when, on 10 July, he was invited to a royal banquet. The king told him not to grieve over the loss of Gower, that he would be reimbursed with lands of equal value, but when the feasting came to a close the king had him arrested and imprisoned. It took a tearful confession to treason for Thomas Beauchamp II to save his life.

The Mowbrays
Mowbray had no sooner been created the first duke of Norfolk than he too fell foul of the king. Early in 1398, Mowbray had quarrelled with Henry Bolingbroke, duke of Lancaster. Both men had agreed to a duel on 16 September, but the king intervened, banishing both men from the realm. A year later, Mowbray died in Venice, of the plague according to one account. In the meantime, Gower had been placed in the custody of the king's escheator, John Skydmore.

En route to Ireland to avenge the death of his proclaimed heir, the Earl of March, Richard II stayed at Sweynesse on 11 and 12 May 1399. According to one of his courtiers, 'the castles of South Wales were totally unfurnished and Richard had to sleep on straw during his sojourn', which was probably the case at Sweynesse. While he was campaigning in Ireland, the exiled Henry Bolingbroke returned to England to lay claim to the throne. Richard arrived back in Pembroke to be abandoned by his favourites, deposed by parliament and imprisoned at Pontefract Castle where he died of starvation the following year.

On 6 December 1399 the new king, Henry IV, founder of the Lancastrian dynasty, appointed a Yorkshireman, Sir Hugh de Waterton, seneschal and receiver of Gower. By a writ dated 20 May 1400, Waterton was ordered to assign a third-part of the lordship to Thomas de Mowbray's widow, Elizabeth, duchess of Norfolk, as her dower. By a document dated 9 July the duchess was assigned several manors, a third of a coal mine worth £30 per annum, and a number of other properties.

A list of her assignments in Sweynesse, which amounted to one third of the borough, coupled with the receiver's account for the year ending Michaelmas 1400, provides valuable information about the town. The burgages allocated to her, for example, were in the hands of 62 burgesses, most of whom bore English names; five of them were women. Only nine burgesses had Welsh names. Some burgesses held more than one burgage—John Fairwood held six and half burgages, John de Horton held five and three-quarters. There were 46 *chensers* (non-burgesses) in the town as a whole. From these figures a number of estimates have been made on the borough's population, ranging from 200 to 1500 persons.

The dowager-duchess's deed provides the names of several streets—St. Mary's Street, High Street, Fisher Street, West Street and Street End. This same document states that West Street led to Sketty and thence to Blackpill; it refers to an orchard which probably gave its name to the present-day Orchard Street. It also mentions a property described as two cellars near the bailey bridge, four shops above the said cellars, two chambers above the shops, all of which were let, yielding a total rent of £1 10s 2d. per annum. This same property is mentioned in an inquisition post-mortem of 1425, only then it is described as one cellar 'next to the bridge of the fortress', four shops and two galleries which, in later years, is believed to have been the town hall. The property stood within the outer bailey, probably against the wall near the unnamed south gate. It is possible that the cellars were at ground level (used as a storerooms), the shops at first floor level, and the galleries may have overlooked the wall in the manner of hording, supported by beams inserted into holes in the bailey wall. From inside the galleries missiles could be directed at attackers. The property appears to have occupied a position in the top end of what is now Castle Gardens.

An account for 1478-9 mentions a parcel of land 'in the Bouteyn', interpreted as Bovetown, meaning 'above the town', and a bye law of 1553 refers to 'the bove town within the north gate'. Some historians have claimed this to be a reference to a suburb that lay to the north of the outer bailey, but the evidence is inconclusive. Even more vague is a reference to 'le denton', meaning 'down town', which is impossible to locate; it was certainly not a southern suburb as has been claimed.

The portreeve (the chief burgess) was supported by the catchpole, whose specific responsibilities were collecting the perquisites of the hundred court and the prise of ale—a tax on brewing; the catchpole for the year ending Michaelmas 1402 doubled up as the castle goaler. The man responsible for the lordship, Sir Hugh de Waterton, held three offices for which he collected three salaries. As seneschal he was responsible for the administration of justice as well as governance; as receiver he was accountable for all revenues and, after deducting expenditure, for delivering the remaining cash to the lord. His third office was that of constable and it becomes clear that, in his day, the castle had no standing garrison, although the holders of fiefs were still obliged to do their castle guard.

On 16 September 1400 rebellion broke out in North Wales when Owain Glyn Dwr, a squire of princely descent, proclaimed himself prince of Wales. Although initially the revolt was confined to North Wales, there was an undercurrent of discontent among the Welsh everywhere at their inequitable treatment by the English. The ministers' account for the year ending Michaelmas 1401 illustrates how serious the authorities viewed the situation. The receiver of Gower, Sir Hugh de Waterton, listed payments for men to clean out the ditches of both the castle and the bailey, and it is significant that only one castle is referred to, presumably because the old castle had fallen into disuse. Money was paid to carpenters, tilers, masons and labourers for repairs to castle buildings, walls and towers. The walls of the outer bailey required considerable attention because, in places, they were 'broken and thrown to the ground', for which lime and sand had to be brought in. A carpenter was commissioned to attend to the two bailey gates, making one anew and repairing the other. A garrison was installed for 28 days during September and October, consisting of three men-at-arms, 'taking each per day 12d', and 18 yeomen archers, 'taking each per day 6d'.

Other security measures involved a payment to two men to take letters from the seneschal to men who would bring together all the knights, esquires and yeomen, sufficient to safeguard Gower at the extreme boundaries—meaning, presumably, the western and northern borders. One of the most interesting entries is a payment made to John David, yeoman, going from Sweynesse to London with a letter of William Stradling, deputy seneschal, to Sir Hugh de Waterton on matters pertaining to the government and custody of Gower, viz., going, staying there and returning, for 14 days, 'taking per day 6d for himself and his horse'. On another occasion John David made a seven-day round trip to Gloucester.

Owain's role as a guerrilla leader was enhanced when, in June 1402, he inflicted a bloody defeat on Herefordshire levies at the Battle of Bryn Glas (Pilleth); from then on, Welshmen flocked to him. The ministers' account for 1401-2 records the response of the authorities at Sweynesse, installing a garrison there for 28 days during July and August, consisting of two men-at-arms and six archers. What made the administrators so nervous was not knowing exactly where Owain was and what he was up to. This is made evident in the ministers' accounts by a payment to two men to spy in the Brecknock/Builth area so that the tenants of Gower might be forewarned against attack. Another garrison was installed for ten days in October, consisting of four men-at-arms and eight archers, because Owain was reported to be rampaging in Brecknock.

No ministers' accounts relating to Gower survive for 1402-3, but the fact that Owain was closing in on Gower is made evident by a letter, dated 5 July 1403, written by John Skydmore, custodian of Carreg Cennen Castle, to John Fairfield, receiver of Brecknock, informing him that the Welsh of 'Carmarthenshire, Cydweli, Carnwyllion and Is-cennen be sworn to Owain yesterday … and on this day he is about Carmarthen and there thinketh to abide till he has the town and castle, and his purpose is hence into Pembrokeshire, for he feels quite sure of all the castles and towns in Cydweli, Gower and Glamorgan [will fall to him], for the [men of those] same countries have undertaken the siege of them until they are won'.

Other letters reveal that Owain had over 8,000 'spears' with which he intimidated garrisons into submission; he also used fifth column tactics to gain access to castles such as Llanstephan, where the custodian, John de Penres, was taken prisoner. (This John de Penres was a member of a cadet branch of the family.) On 6 July, Owain took Carmarthen by surprise, killing more than 50 townspeople, burning the town and forcing the castle's custodian to yield. It was while he was at Carmarthen that Owain sent for Hopcyn ap Thomas of Ynysdawy in the Tawe Valley. A cultured collector of manuscripts, renown for his knowledge of bardic law, Hopcyn was considered an authority of bardic prophecies and now prophesied that Owain would soon be taken prisoner somewhere between Carmarthen and Gower, which is supposed to have deterred Owain from advancing on the lordship.

A month later, Owain had carried the war into Glamorgan and must, therefore, have passed through Gower. Tradition has it that he did not lay siege to any castles within the lordship because the men of Gower, both English and Welsh, had 'undertaken the siege of them' for him. This is supported in part by negative evidence from an inquisition post mortem of Thomas Mowbray II in 1410, which records the value of Mowbray's two-thirds of Gower as only £100 per annum due to the devastation caused by the *rebelles Wallensium*. That same year the inquisition post mortem of Sir John de la Bere found the manor of Weobley to be likewise of no value beyond reprises due to frequent assaults by the Welsh.

Although these sources only refer to damage done by the Welsh, it is possible that English tenants were involved in the revolt because they, like the Welsh, were tired of administrators who tried to squeeze from them every penny that was due in the form of rents and amercements. Indeed, elsewhere, English tenants often defected to the rebel camp in order to safeguard themselves from attack.

Whatever happened in Gower during the weeks before Owain appeared in Glamorgan it is certain that Sweynesse did not fall to the rebels because, on 12 September, the king granted Peter Courtenay and others a commission to take 20 quarters of wheat, 3 tons of wine, 8 tons of ale, 1,000 fish, and 20 quarters of oats to the town and castle of Sweynesse. On 28 September, John Zely of Llanstephan was granted a safe-passage to sail to England and Ireland to buy victuals 'for the sustenance of soldiers and others dwelling in the castle and town of Sweynesse'. Unlike Kidwelly, which withstood a three-year siege, Sweynesse is likely to have fallen to the rebels, but the castle may have been only damaged, not destroyed, for in 1417 a later Mowbray made reference to 'our castle of Sweynesse'.

No more is heard of Sweynesse until after 1406 when, according to the *Annales of Owain Glyn Dwr*, the men of Gower made their submissions to the king's agents. These submissions were obviously made by Welshmen, presumably those of *Wallicana*, for on 26 June 1405 the king had confirmed the charter of 1306 to the men of the English county, which suggests that by June 1405 the Englishry must have been in the king's hands. By then, Owain had suffered a major defeat near Usk; it was the turning point of the war.

Despite the uncertainty surrounding Gower during the height of the Glyn Dwr rebellion, Thomas Mowbray II had been granted seisin of his inheritance in November 1403, including two-thirds of Gower. His tenure proved short-lived, for his involvement in Archbishop Scrope's northern rebellion cost him his head in June 1405, and once again two-thirds of Gower became Crown property. Between June 1405 and 1437 Gower changed hands on numerous occasions—often it was held by the Crown, sometimes by the Mowbrays, by a second dowager-duchess (Catherine, duchess of Norfolk) and by a duke of Buckingham.

In 1417 a burgage was granted to a Roger Joudrell who, three years later, as receiver of Gower, reported a scarcity of wheat and other cereals to the extent that the people could not make sufficient bread for their needs, being forced to obtain bread from elsewhere, or to eat flesh during times of fasting. As a result, Roger was commissioned by the king to purchase 200 quarters of beans from Somerset and Dorset and ship them to Sweynesse from Bristol and Berkeley.

A writ was issued on 20 August 1435, ordering an inquisition post mortem on the possessions held by the late Richard Mansel, lord of Nicholaston. Richard's son, Hugh, had married Isabella, daughter of John de Penres, grandson of the Robert de Penres who died post-1336. It is possible that John de Penres was succeeded for a short while (c.1436-7) by his son, another John, whose untimely death led to the Penres estate (the fiefs of Penres, Oxwich, Port Eynon, Llangenydd and divers other places) passing to Hugh Mansel as a result of his marriage to Isabella. Thus, after some 300 years, the line of Penres was superseded by a family that would have no small part to play in the history of Gower.

Another John Mowbray, the third duke of Norfolk, reached maturity in 1436. It was during the tenure of this turbulent man, who was twice imprisoned in the Tower, that Llangenydd's existence as an alien priory finally ended. As a result of the Hundred Years War the priory had been seized by the Crown in 1414, and in 1440 its lands and advowson, including Pennard Church, were transferred to All Saints College, Oxford. The hermitage of St. Kenydd-atte-Holme is several times mentioned in the 15th century, the king granting it to named hermits in 1429, 1439, 1442 and 1482.

It was during John Mowbray III's tenure that Sweynesse's earliest acclaimed hero, Sir Hugh Johnys, flourished, although he was not born in Gower. Like all the Welsh gentry of his day Sir Hugh claimed descent from someone of princely birth—in his case it was Maenarch, a late 11th century lord of Brycheiniog. His father, John, was the son of Watkin Vaughan, son of Sir Roger Vaughan who fell at Agincourt in 1415.

According to his brass memorial, which can be seen in St. Mary's Church, Sir Hugh became a knight of the Holy Sepulchre in Jerusalem on 14 August 1441, after devoting five years to fighting in 'Troy, Greece and Turkey'. At a slightly later date he became knight marshal of France for his services there. By June 1446 he was serving in the household of 'the good John [Mowbray], duke of Norfolk', possibly as a chamberlain, under whose patronage he was appointed knight marshal of England.

Sir Hugh came to Gower to become the duke's chief administrator. In 1451 he was appointed constable of Oystermouth Castle, steward of the manor of Oystermouth, and surveyor and approver[a] of the lordship, receiving the attendant fee for each office. The duke made sure that Sir Hugh would want for nothing, granting him 40 acres of demesne land at Oystermouth and, in December 1451, granting him Landimore which, alone, provided him with an income of more than £50 a year. He also had a property at Ye Goedre, near Hendrefoilan, though by what means is unknown.

As a young man, Sir Hugh had desired to marry the beautiful Elizabeth Woodville, later to become the queen of Edward IV. He eventually married a local girl, Maud, daughter of Rees Cradock. This marriage must have taken place before 1460 because, in that year, both he and Maud were granted a tenement in Fisher Street (now lower Princess Way) in Sweynesse. Maud bore him at least nine children. He died sometime after 1485, his body taken to St. Mary's Church where a brass memorial marked the place of his interment and that of his wife.

The Herberts of Raglan

The Wars of the Roses had been fought intermittently for almost a decade when, in March 1461, the late arrival of Duke Mowbray III's forces at the Battle of Towton proved decisive in deposing the insane Lancastrian king, Henry VI, in

The Hugh Johnys brass, St. Mary's Church, the plaque beneath the figures recording his titles to fame

[a]The duties of an approver were to collect the heriots (a form of death duties) from tenants, both free and customary, usually the best beast, which were due to the lord. In later times the office was combined with that of the clerk of court (first mentioned in the ministers' account of 1401-2), the responsibilities of which were to record court proceedings and take charge of the chancery where all records were kept.

favour of the Yorkist king, Edward IV. When Duke Mowbray died later that same year, his heir was still a minor and the Mowbray inheritance, including Gower, came under the wardship of Edward. There were many Lancastrian supporters among the gentry of Gower, the most notable being Philip Mansel of Oxwich, and to safeguard his interests the king granted custody of the lordship to his most trusted supporter, William, Lord Herbert of Raglan, on 12 February 1462. As justiciar of South Wales Lord Herbert quickly subdued the Lancastrian supporters in West Wales, ousted Jasper Tudor from Pembroke and took control of all forfeited lands. By 1467 he had gained control of almost the whole of Wales as well as huge estates in England; in 1468 he became earl of Pembroke, the first Welshman to become a peer.

The young John Mowbray took possession of his inheritance in March 1465, becoming the fourth duke of Norfolk. Yet Lord Herbert retained control of Gower and, in the autumn of 1468, he prevailed upon Duke John to give him Gower and Chepstow in exchange for lands in East Anglia. Lord Herbert's days of aggrandizement came to an abrupt end due to a successful rebellion in July 1469, which resulted in the temporary imprisonment of Edward IV; Herbert was beheaded that same month.

Gower was once again held by the Crown until Lord Herbert's son, William II, reached maturity in 1475, but William II, through his inadequacy, lost much of his West Wales inheritance, including the earldom of Pembroke, and by 1479 the king's second son was styling himself lord of Gower. William II may have recovered Gower in 1482, if only temporarily, for in 1483 it was again Crown property.

Documentary evidence shows that, throughout the later half of the 15th century, Sweynesse continued to prosper, especially in the cloth trade. The receiver's account for 1400 mentions a fulling mill where cloth was cleansed and thickened; by 1449 there were four if not five such mills in the town, and by 1478 there was a smelting house near the castle. Ships' cargoes provide information on trade: in 1447 the owners of the 80 ton *Mary of Sweynesse* were given a licence to sail from Bristol to Iceland with goods and bring back fish, whereas in 1499 the *Vincent of Guernsey* arrived in Sweynesse with Rochelle wine, cards and white paper, and also Guernsey cloth, canvas and chamlet (a kind of cloth).

The Somersets

William, Lord Herbert II died in July 1490, leaving his daughter, Elizabeth, and his brother, Sir Walter Herbert, to dispute his estate. In June 1492, Elizabeth married Sir Charles Somerset, and with his help she gained possession of the greater part of her inheritance in Wales, including Gower. When Sir Walter died in September 1507, Sir Charles took over his estate, adopting the title of Lord Herbert of Raglan, Chepstow and Gower. These estates, along with the custodianship of Glamorgan, made Sir Charles a powerful figure in South Wales, even more so when, in 1514, he received the title of earl of Worcester.

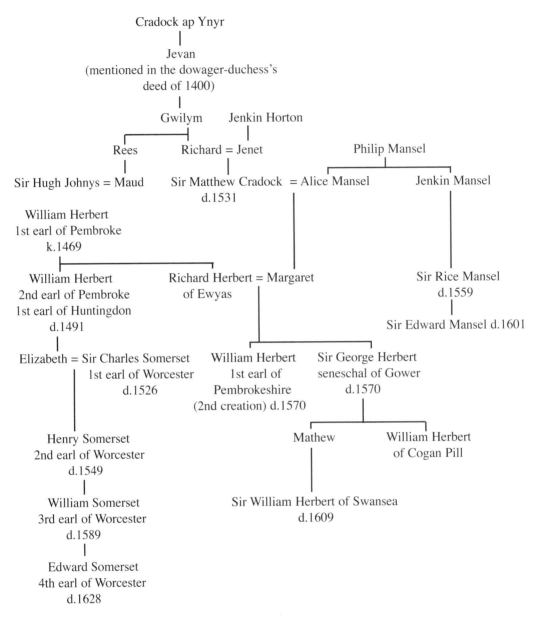

The Somerset/Herbert/Cradock/Mansel connections

Men such as Sir Charles may have held Gower of the king, but the people who really held sway over the lordship were the seneschals, some of whom were despots. The earliest seneschal of whom a great deal is known is Sir Matthew Cradock, who came from a family of prominent burgesses.[b] In 1498 he was appointed seneschal and receiver of Gower, constable of Sweynesse Castle and chancellor (which made him responsible for the chancery). He received £10 per annum for the office of

A model of the Plas, probably built by Sir Mathew Cradock in the early 16th century. It was demolished in 1840

seneschal and £3 6s 8d for each of the other offices. By 1500 he was Sir Charles's lieutenant in Glamorgan—deputy sheriff of the lordship Glamorgan (the Vale) and seneschal of Morgannwg (the uplands).

A patron of the bards and a substantial landowner in Gower and Glamorgan, Sir Matthew was also a shrewd businessman, purchasing a lease for 80 years, in 1526, of all the coal mines in Gower for only £11. His immense wealth enabled him to build the magnificent mansion known as the Plas, or Place, within the south-western corner of the outer bailey, now Castle Gardens. Access to the Plas was by way of an arch, bearing the family crest and the motto 'the Place I take' is a reference to the *placeam bugagii* of 1383. The approach road to the house later became known as Temple Street.

Sir Matthew married twice, his first wife being Alice, sister of Sir Rice Mansel. Before he died in 1531 he arranged for a magnificent stone tomb to be constructed and placed in St. Ann's Chapel in St. Mary's Church, hoping that he and his second

---

[b]The family claimed descent from Einion ap Collwyn, an apocryphal prince connected with the Norman Conquest of Glamorgan. Sir Matthew's great-grandfather, Jevan ap Cradock, was one of the nine Welsh burgesses mentioned in the dowager-duchess's assignment of 1400. Jevan (Evan) is reputed to have killed a huge, wild boar in the forest of Clyne, the reason why the boar's head became part of the family crest. Sir Matthew's father, Richard, was one of several brothers to adopt Cradock as a surname. His mother, Jenet, was the daughter of Jenkin Horton, descendant of the John Horton who had been granted a 'place burgage' in 1383, and from her, Sir Matthew inherited the compact group of burgages mentioned in the deed of 1383.

wife, Catherine Gordon, might share a common grave. Unfortunately, Catherine outlived him long enough to remarry twice, being buried in Berkshire. Even more unfortunate, the beautifully inscribed tomb suffered irreparable damage as a result of bombing during the Second World War.

Sir Charles died in 1526 to be succeeded in all things, including the custodianship of Glamorgan, by his son, Henry. Unlike his father, Earl Henry is known to have visited Gower on at least one occasion, for in a letter to the king, dated 21 January 1527, he refers to a visit during the previous year in which he made an attempt to apprehend certain murderers and felons who were residing in the lordship. Much to his disgust the felons gained sanctuary, being forewarned by the men of those parts. (A second visit may have taken place in 1534 when a payment was recorded for cleaning the stables of Sweynesse Castle 'against my lord's coming'.)

1527 was the year in which Sir Matthew Cradock retired from holding office and, although acquisitive, he appears to have been an able administrator, but his grandson, George Herbert, who succeeded him in all his offices, soon proved himself to be a despot. Herbert's maladministration led to friction between himself and the tenants of Gower; this culminated in an indenture, dated 1 September 1532, in which the earl, in return for 350 marks, agreed to confirm the charter of 1306. Specific clauses in the indenture provide the clues as to what Herbert and his officers had been up to.

It would appear that everyone in the lordship had cause to complain. One of the grievances of the Swansea burgesses, for instance, relates to their original 12th-century charter, which prescribed a 40s fine on all 'outsiders' who drew blood on a Sunday, whereas Herbert had been imposing the fine on the burgesses as well. In the Welshry the tenants complained that Herbert and his officers were anything but impartial when it came to levying aids called *cymorthau*. Some tenants in the lordship alleged that, when officers made false accusations against them, Herbert had failed to deal with their complaints in the prescribed way. Others had complained of Herbert's failure to punish certain persons who had wrongfully dispossessed them of their lands, or that Herbert himself had unjustly dispossessed them of their tenements.

Many of the clauses in the indenture deal with issues that highlight the commercial activities in Sweynesse—for example, in future, the seneschal, on receiving a complaint from the portreeve, had to evict all artificers who practised 'cutting and carving' (probably shoemakers and saddlers) within a 7-mile radius of the town, excepting those who lived within the town. It would appear that those who objected to 'outsiders' exercising such crafts were the tradesmen who lived within the town and who paid 'scotage and tallage'. Another clause relating to the demands of what must surely have been a guild of tanners was one which called for the appointment of two burgesses to inspect all leather brought into the town. If the leather was found to be not properly tanned, then it was confiscated and the 'outside' tanner fined. The indenture stated that smiths and tailors were excluded from the expulsion; it also confirmed the burgesses' right to sell wool anywhere in the realm without hindrance by the seneschal and his officers.

Despite the problems caused by his maladministration, Herbert continued to hold all his offices in Gower, Glamorgan and Morgannwg. This may have been due, in part, to the likelihood that it suited Henry Somerset to keep him in his employ. It must surely have had something to do with Herbert's family connections, he being related to Henry Somerset and to all the Herberts who held sway over much of South Wales. Herbert's mother, Margaret, was the daughter and heiress of Sir Matthew Cradock, and it is through her that he inherited Sir Matthew's estate, including the Plas where he resided.

A growing concern for Henry VIII was the rise in lawlessness in Wales. The Council in the March, based at Ludlow, had powers to deal with the disorder, but had proved ineffectual. One of the problems was that there were too many Marcher lordships, which made it easy for felons to evade capture in one lordship simply by taking refuge in another. It was said that lawlessness was at its worse in the numerous lordships that were in the custody of Henry Somerset, whose officers were all too often guilty of malpractice. In a memorandum of 1533-4 a member of the Council, Thomas Holte, reported that murder and cattle-stealing often went unpunished because, if any gentleman or mischievous person committed murder, or was arrested for theft, they obtained a pardon by paying a fine to the officers in charge of the petty lordship; then they recovered their money by levying a *cymorth* on the king's poorer subjects.

Tomb of Sir Matthew Cradock and Lady Catherine Gordon as it stood in Swansea Church before it was damaged by bombing in the Second World War

Holte's criticisms of the Welsh gentry, who were forever increasing in number due to the custom of partible inheritance, is borne out by a statement made in 1524 by Sir Matthew Cradock to the effect that, in Gower, men of 'small substance' often demanded a *cymorth* from their tenants to offset gifting their daughters in marriage, or for carrying out repairs on their houses. Sir Matthew also alleged that the tenants, fearing to displease these gentlemen and their relatives and friends, gave an animal, corn or money to their own impoverishment.

That is not to say that felons were never hanged. If a felon did not have the means to purchase a pardon, then he ended up on the gallows to be suspended indefinitely. This deplorable state of affairs could easily be exacerbated by miscarriages of justice, such as the one referred to in Holte's memorandum. The wording used by Holte suggests quite strongly that the matter he referred to took place at Sweynesse where a 16-year-old youth had been imprisoned in the castle. Holte stated that George Herbert, seneschal of Gower, had arrested a rich man's son dwelling 'thereby' and charged him with stealing a ship from his own father, which the father utterly denied. Yet the young man was made to confess the felony. Herbert then ordered the father to bring 'a grett some of money, or else his son should be hanged'. The father complained to the Council, whereupon, the Council sent a letter to Herbert commanding him to postpone the execution till the matter had been investigated, but Herbert had the youth hanged and threatened to hang the father as well.

Writing on behalf of the Council, Holte made several recommendations as to how to tackle the problem of lawlessness, but the king proved non-committal until after the break with Rome in 1534. Then, on 1 July 1536, an act was passed which abolished the regal jurisdiction of the Marcher lords; henceforth law was upheld in the name of the king. This led to the 'Act of Laws and Justice to be ministered in Wales in like form as it is in this realm', which later became known as the Act of Union. By this means Wales became part of England, its laws becoming English laws, and the Marcher lordships were to be grouped together to form counties, which put the Marcher lords on the same footing as those lords who held land only in England.

Gower would have been incorporated into the enlarged county of Carmarthen but for the fact that Henry Somerset, who held Gower of the king, also held the sheriffdom of the lordship of Glamorgan and the stewardship of Morgannwg. As the king had no wish to upset Henry so these three areas were amalgamated to form the new county of Glamorgan. It took a transitional period of several years for these reforms to be implemented; it was not until 17 November 1540 that the first sheriff of the new county was appointed—none other than George Herbert. The following year, Herbert was knighted, then elected to be the first knight of the shire to represent Glamorgan in Parliament. The transitional period ended in 1543 when an act was passed to abolish gravelkind.

CHAPTER VII
Union & Civil War

Early in 1536, Henry VIII ordered the suppression of all monasteries worth less than £200 and, in August, Margam Abbey was dissolved and its estates placed in the custody of Sir Rice Mansel of Oxwich. Four years later Sir Rice purchased most of the abbey's estates, becoming the richest landowner in Gower and Glamorgan. Sir George Herbert also benefited from the dissolution, acquiring several monastic estates in the Cardiff area. Both men benefitted yet again from the dissolution of the Order of St. John (the Hospitallers) in 1540. Then, in 1548, following a decision to dissolve all chantries, hospitals and free chapels, Herbert acquired the endowments of the Hospital of St. David in Sweynesse to become the second wealthiest man in Gower and to be numbered amongst the five richest in Glamorgan.

In the late Born in 1487, Sir Rice Mansel, who became the most prominent landowner in Gower, spent many years in the care of his uncle, Sir Mathew Cradock, with whom he served at sea in 1509, having charge of two vessels. After succeeding to his inheritance in 1510 he built Oxwich Castle, a six-storeyed fortified mansion, the ruins of which can be seen today. As a senior officer he served in Flanders in 1517 and in Ireland in 1535; he was knighted before 1526. It was through his third wife, Cecily, who had been a lady-in-waiting to Princess Mary, that his influence in royal circles peaked, marching at the head of 500 men at Mary's coronation in 1553. That same year he became chamberlain and chancellor of South Wales.

In the late 1530s, John Leland wrote his *Itinerary in Wales*, though whether he actually visited Gower, or relied upon correspondents to provide him with information is unknown. What he wrote about Gower is not very informative and riddled with inaccuracies, but he did mention that 'Sweynesse is a market town' – not a very pleasant one apparently, for an Act of Parliament of 1544 states: 'in times past' there had been 'many beautifully houses' within the walls of Sweynesse that have become 'fallen down and decayed … many of them adjoining' the main streets and filled 'with much odour, filth and uncleanliness, with their pits, cellars and vaults lying open and uncovered'. The town, like any other, must have been littered with refuse, a breeding ground for rats, for one of the earliest surviving ordinances of the borough, dated 1553, states that 'no man or woman, nor their servants, shall throw dung nor filth from their houses or streets in any place on the strand side except outside the bounds laid down by the portreeve and aldermen'. The aldermen were twelve co-opted members of the town council.

For judicial purposes the Act of Union led to the division of Gower into two hundreds—Sweynesse and Llangyfelach—reflecting the old Welsh divisions of Is-coed and Uwch-coed. The Act also made the people of Gower liable to pay taxes to the Crown whilst, at the same time, they continued to pay whatever was due to their lord. The first tax assessment took place in 1543-4, the tax being levied on all heads of households except those who were too poor, such as domestics, labourers and paupers. The assessment has often been used to provide population estimates, based on the assumption that each taxpayer represented a household of five persons.

In Sweynesse there were 111 taxpayers, although the number of households is usually presented as 130 to allow for non-taxpayers; this represents approximately 650 persons, about half of whom were the burgesses and their families. In Loughor there were only 15 taxpayers. Almost 20 years years later the bishop of St. David's returns gave a rough estimate of the number of households in the deanery of Gower; multiplied by five they suggest a population as follows:

Sweynesse town	180 households	900 persons
Sweynesse hundred	736 households	3,680 persons
Llangyfelach hundred	437 households	2,185 persons
Total:	1,353 households	5,865 persons

85% of taxpayers (about 1,000 persons) were probably classed as 'husbandmen'—small-time farmers, rural craftsmen and shopkeepers. Most of the remainder were yeomen farmers who, as freeholders, were permitted to serve as jurors. Only a minority of taxpayers could be considered gentry, many of whom were also leading burgesses. Knights there were, but only members of the Mansel and the Herbert families were knighted with any regularity. The only peer, the biggest landowner of all, was the earl of Worcester.

In 1557, differences between Sir George Herbert and the Mansels turned to violence, the spark provided by a French ship which ran aground in Oxwich Bay, its crew barely making it ashore. Two days later, Sir George Herbert rode up to Oxwich Castle with an armed posse, intending to lay claim to the cargo and crew on behalf of the earl of Worcester who, as lord of Gower, had a right to all wrecks. Outside the gates he was confronted by Sir Rice Mansel's son, Edward, and in the affray which followed, Edward's aunt, Ann Mansel, was killed by a stone thrown by one of Herbert's men. Sir Rice, who was not in residence during the affray, brought an action against Herbert and his men on charges of riot and forcible entry; they were all found guilty and later stood trial for the killing of Ann Mansel. Herbert and his

Oxwich Castle—the gateway was once the scene of an affray in which Ann Mansel was killed by a stone

men were ordered to pay restitution, while the man who had thrown the stone was eventually pardoned.

Herbert died in 1570, but ten years earlier his successor as seneschal had been none other than Edward Mansel. He proved to be incompetent, but Earl William presumably put up with him due to the fact that they were brother-in-laws. By 1580, Earl William, who had succeeded his father in the 1550s, had become convinced that, from about 1560 onwards, his tenants in Gower had made widespread encroachments on his pastures, meadows and woodland. It was later claimed by William's son, Edward, that as a result of a survey carried out in 1583 this had begun as a result of his tenants digging furze for fuel in certain areas to the exclusion of all others, gradually enclosing the land with hedges and fences. This was part of a widespread development towards enclosure, the result of a gradual disappearance, in the 16th century, of the manorial system of cultivation with its emphasis on open fields and obligations to the lord in favour of rent-paying tenants, many of whom feared encroachment on their land by their neighbours.

Trade had been expanding in the coastal areas around South Wales throughout the 16th century and with it came an increase in piratical activity. The pirates were invariably native to the region, some of them influential men; even Sir Mathew Cradock may have been involved in piracy. The pirates preyed on foreign ships usually, favouring cargos such as salt and wine—those which were either necessities, or carried high levels of tax. After sailing a captured vessel into port the pirates sold off its cargo at knock-down prices, often bribing officials in the process.

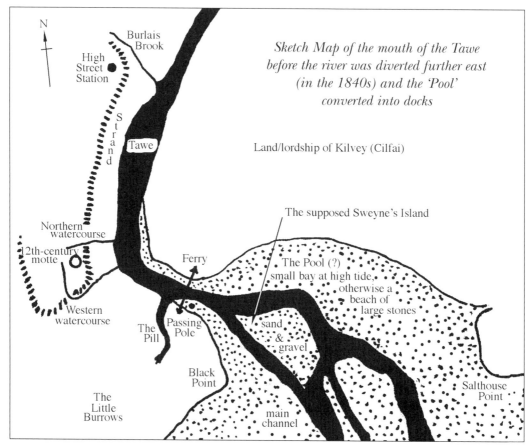

Sketch Map of the mouth of the Tawe before the river was diverted further east (in the 1840s) and the 'Pool' converted into docks

N

Burlais Brook

High Street Station

Strand

Tawe

Land/lordship of Kilvey (Cilfai)

The supposed Sweyne's Island

Northern watercourse

12th-century motte

Ferry

The Pool (?) small bay at high tide, otherwise a beach of large stones

Western watercourse

The Pill

Passing Pole

sand & gravel

Black Point

Salthouse Point

The Little Burrows

main channel

One such incident appears to have taken place in 1581 when a London ship, the *Primrose*, sailed into Swanzey[a] with a cargo of Brazilian wood, cotton, peppers, parrots and monkeys. The two piracy commissioners who were called in, one of them Sir William Herbert, were prepared to accept the captain's implausible explanation as to how he had acquired the cargo and were happy to accept a monkey apiece. The customs officer had been presented with two parrots which, he subsequently claimed, had died two weeks later. Throughout their stay in Swanzey the ship's crew came ashore daily to 'make merry in sundry places', behaving themselves 'civilly' according to the customs officer. It was only after the ship had left Swanzey that the real owner of the cargo, a Frenchman, managed to have the crew and the customs officer brought before a judge in London. Unfortunately, the outcome of the case is not known.

The *Common Hall Book*, records, in 1585, 'the Shirehall of Swanzey being almost finished' at a cost of £60 without giving any indication as to where it stood, or what

---

[a]Swansea has over 80 variations in its spelling. Swanzey first appeared in an entry in the Common Hall Book for the year 1555; from then on it became the usual form of spelling for the town's name.

it looked like. This has led to controversy among local historians because a deed of 1583 mentions a town house 'adjoining on the one side to the garden of Sir William Herbert [presumably part of the Plas] and the street called the Market Place on the other side', which corresponds to the property mentioned in 1400 and 1425 where the burgesses are believed to have held their meetings. The receivers' account for 1478-9 refers to a 'county house called the Shirehall' where legal proceeding took place. Whether the Shirehall of 1585 is the Townhall-cum-Shirehall that is frequently mentioned in the 1640s is unclear. If these buildings were one and the same, then the castle—which was described in Somerset's survey of 1583 as 'in decay'—must have been partially demolished, its western defences removed to make way for the construction of the Shirehall of 1585. This may well have been the case as the castle had to some extent been rendered obsolete by the the Act of Union and the abolition of castle guard during the time of Henry VIII. Alternatively, the Townhall and the Shirehall may have been, prior to the 1640s, two separate buildings because, between 1618 and 1646, the burgesses were still paying rent for 'the Town House in the Market Place'.[1]

Apart from its use as a meeting place, the Townhouse was used for storage, a fact confirmed by an ordinance of 1555 which states that all goods coming into the port, except perishables, were to be taken to the Townhall where they were to remain in the custody of the common attorneys (two officials who served as borough treasurers) for 15 days till the burgesses had purchased whatever they required, after which the non-burgesses could purchase any remaining goods.

An ordinance dated 1583 ordered that all ships or boats, before going up to the coal or landing place, had to discharge their ballast on the Perroge by the Pill in places appointed by an official called the layer-keeper. This was both to prevent the Tawe from becoming blocked and to facilitate the use of ballast as building material. The Perroge (then recently built) is the earliest known quay on the river bank, its location being near the Passing Pole where the portreeve, or his deputy, boarded all ships entering the port to inspect the cargo and levy tolls if necessary. After discharging the ballast—except that which was retained to 'bear their mast'— the ships proceeded to the coal or landing place where they discharged their cargos and remaining ballast.

The coal or landing place extended along the strand, north of the Perroge where, at ebb tide, the ships lay in the mud. Coal had become an important component of trade to the south-west of England, France, Ireland and the Channel Islands for use in homes, iron smelting and lime burning. There were coal mines dotted all over Gower by 1585, from Llansamlet in the east to Llanrhidian in the west, from Gwaun-Caegurwen in the far north to Oystermouth in the south.

After William Somerset died in 1589 his son, Edward, was forced to engage in lengthy litigation, claiming that in Gower more than 3,000 acres had been illegally enclosed, but his tenants contested his claims, in some instances to the point of rioting. In 1595, Edward brought a bill of complaint against 80 named tenants, the worst offenders being Sir William Herbert (grandson of Sir George Herbert) and his tenants and farmers whom, he claimed, had enclosed more than 500 acres. He also brought a complaint in general terms against the whole tenantry, about 1,000 persons. These claims of enclosure, together with claims for aids which the tenants had refused to pay, were dismissed out of court, probably because the jury had been made up of men who were themselves guilty of encroachment.

Mention has been made to the market place outside the southern gate of the outer bailey. In his *Morganiae Archaiographia*, published in 1578, Rice Merrick stated that market day fell once weekly on a Saturday as it does to this very day. Merrick also referred to the three yearly fairs, the churchwardens' account for 1599 recording that the fairs were held in St. Mary's churchyard, the stands occupied by hatters, peddlers and glovers (who are known to have had their own private chapel in the church).

A variety of early 17th-century documents provide a list of the occupations of those who lived and worked in the town. Those who dealt with food and drink included bakers, brewers, butchers, fishmongers, inn-keepers, millers, victuallers and vintners. The clothing trade is represented by buttonmakers, cappers, dyers, feltmakers, hatters, mercers, seamstresses, tailors, tuckers and weavers. Leatherworkers included cobblers, curriers, glovers, saddlers, shoemakers and tanners. In the building trade there were carpenters, glaziers, joiners, masons, paviers, plumbers and tilers. Other craftsmen included barbers, cutlers, hoopers, pewterers, shipbuilders, smiths and tinkers. There were doctors, clergymen and lawyers, merchants and peddlers, colliers and ironworkers, mariners, husbandmen, yeomen and labourers. There were also office-bearers who were answerable to either the seneschal or the portreeve.

It appears that Edward Somerset never recovered the land inclosed by his tenants, but he continued to lay claim to what he considered to be his dues, and in 1601 an assessment was made towards the payment of a feudal due called mises. Out of the 137 Swanzey residents who appear in the assessment 71 can be regarded as low wage-earners or husbandmen which, in many instances, amounted to much the same thing, for a collier named John Boycott died in 1613, leaving a cow, a heifer, two calves and a horse.

The wealthiest man in town was Sir William Herbert who resided at the Plas, but the most interesting man among the top 10% of those assessed was John Moris, gentleman, who had been sworn a burgess in 1586, elected an alderman in 1593 and became deputy portreeve in 1598. Moris appears to have been no gentleman in the modern sense of the word, being disfranchised on 24 September 1588 for buying for himself a whole shipload of salt, contrary to the by-laws of the town; he was, however, re-admitted to the freedom of the borough that same day on payment of a 6s. fine. In 1601 he and his wife, Johan, were involved in a dispute over the use of a pew in St. Mary's Church, arbitration eventually leading to both parties agreeing to share the pew.

When he died in 1608, Moris's possessions were valued at £322 2s. 1d. According to the inventory compiled after his death his house, unique in that it had glazed windows, consisted of a hall, parlour, seven chambers, a shop, buttery, kitchen and cellar. His furniture and fittings included a Turkish carpet, a Spanish bed, taffeta curtains, a large looking glass, a drawing table, carved and embroidered chairs, to say nothing of silver plates and spoons and a great deal of clothing.

If there is one thing Moris had in common with the collier mentioned above, it is that he kept livestock—in his case 47 cattle, 16 horses and 78 sheep—as well as corn and hay. Almost every inventory of the early 17th century highlights the fact that, no matter what their occupation, the majority of the townspeople kept livestock, which they grazed on Cefn Coed, Townhill and the Burrows (the low-lying wasteland between the Tawe and the Brynmill Stream); almost as many people stored grain. The town must, therefore, have comprised of not only houses, but barns, stables and cowsheds, as well as gardens for growing vegetables, and the streets must have been strewn with dung.

It has been suggested that by subtracting the 137 householders mentioned in the 1601 assessment from the 180 household(er)s referred to in the bishop's returns of 1563, it would appear that at least 43 householders in Swanzey were too poor to contribute to the mises of 1601. What is very apparent, judging by the names that appear in a variety of early 17th-century documents, is that more than half the town's population were either Welsh, or of Welsh extraction, and this applied as much to the burgesses as to *chensers*, a fact confirmed in 1593 when the vicar of St. Marys was upbraided for failing to conduct some of his services in Welsh. This change over to a predominantly Welsh population had taken place gradually during the 15th century and then accelerated following the Act of Union.

Edward Somerset died in 1628 to be succeeded by his son, Henry, by which time Swanzey had two more quays and a dock had been constructed by 1624, its exact location unknown. By 1630 it becomes evident that iron was being shipped from Swanzey in considerable quantities to Bristol (107 tons) and Barnstaple (12 tons).

In 1631 payments were made by the Swanzey Corporation for repairs to the school house that occupied the hall and loft of the townhouse, although there is no evidence that the Corporation was responsible for the day-to-day running of the school. Rice Merrick mentioned the existence of a school at Swanzey, but gave no details as to where it stood, or by what means it was maintained, and there is nothing to suggest that this school and the one mentioned in 1631 were one and the same. The churchwardens' account for 1584 records that a master paid rent for a house which, presumably, belonged to the church which, in turn, suggests that the school, or at least the one referred to by Merrick, was in private hands.

The Civil War

When Henry VIII broke with Rome he unwittingly set in motion a movement to reform the Church. In the decades that followed, both the Crown and the Church of England were prepared to make some changes, but there were those who protested (Protestants) that the changes did not go far enough. By the time of Queen Elizabeth the extremists (the Puritans) were seeking to purify the Church of all trace of Catholicism, desiring a simpler form of worship with the emphasis on preaching.

The earliest record of puritanism in Gower is connected with a Neath man who, in 1580, bequeathed money for the preaching of sermons in Welsh at Llangyfelach and Swanzey, locations that were to become centres of Puritan ideas, more so Swanzey because of its trade links with Bristol and London where puritanism had taken root. From 1613 onwards the accounts of the Swanzey common attorneys record payments to itinerant preachers, and the parish register shows a growing preference for biblical names in the 1630s.

There was, however, one other enclave where Puritan ideas had germinated—the parishes of Penmaen and Pennard—for in 1636 it was reported that the vicar of Penmaen, Marmaduke Matthew, had preached 'against the keeping of all holy days'. When faced with court proceedings in 1638, Matthew fled to New England where he became a preacher. In the adjoining parish of Pennard the parishioners had, in April 1642, urged the authorities to appoint a Flintshire man, Ambrose Mostyn, to be their 'lecturer' because he was 'of goodly sort, and one who can preach in the Welsh and English tongues', but he had to flee to England after the outbreak of civil war.

Of the laity with Puritan sympathies Philip Jones stands apart from all others in that he became one of the most controversial figures ever to have been raised in Gower.[2] Jones left Gower shortly after the outbreak of hostilities to become comptroller (financial officer) of Oliver Cromwell's household, attaining the rank of colonel. On his return he not only became seneschal of Gower, but because of his rise to a position of power and influence throughout South Wales, coupled perhaps with his Puritan sympathies, he was frequently accused of cowardice, corruption and negligence of duty, though nothing was ever proved. One man who remained in Gower to be persecuted for his Puritan sympathies was Rowland Dawkin of Kilvrough, a landowner in the parish of Pennard, whose three daughters were all given biblical names. Sometime after September 1643, Dawkin left Gower to take a commission in the parliamentary army; he eventually attained the rank of a major-general.

There were undoubtedly Puritan sympathizers in Swanzey, but by and large the people of Gower were unaffected by Puritan ideology. Little wonder, then, that when Charles I raised his standard at Nottingham on 22 August 1642, Swanzey and Gower declared for the king, as did most of Wales, for it was said by one eminent Puritan that the common people 'did follow the gentry and [they] were for the king'. In Gower the gentry may have been influenced by the fact that their lord, Henry Somerset—who had become the first marquis of Worcester—had also declared for the king, although Somerset's influence was marginal, being an absentee landlord.

Another factor to be considered is the position of the seneschal. For over 30 years—from 1601 or earlier—the seneschal of Gower had been Sir Thomas Mansel of Oxwich and Margam. After Sir Thomas's death in 1631, Walter Thomas of Dan-y-graig, a Swanzey mercer and merchant who claimed descent from Einion ap Collwyn and who had twice been portreeve, became deputy-seneschal. Following the outbreak of war he was appointed governor of Swanzey, the man in charge of the garrison. He was also a commissioner of array; as such it fell to him to impress men into the county militia, or trained band, which he did in such numbers that, when pressed for more men in the summer of 1643, he complained that Gower had been 'so gleaned of all spare people with these several occasions [in which there had been a call for more men] that the husbandmen will be hardly able to manage their tillage'.

Apart from meeting the demands for men and money, Thomas had instructions to make Swanzey an arsenal. The common attorneys' account for 1642 records expenses 'in making of the new magazine in the lower Townhall', which involved converting a storage room on the ground floor. Then, on 24 July 1643, the authorities at Cardiff entered into an agreement with two Frenchmen to deliver to Swanzey: '200 barrels of powder, two parts being musket powder and one part cannon at 18d. per pound, 1,000 pounds of match at 6d. per pound, and 500 li muskets and bandoliers at 18p [per] musket and bandolier'. The Frenchmen were obviously worried about Parliamentary warships because it was agreed that, in the event of mischance, they were to be compensated for any loss. This gunrunning escapade may have been one of several, for in a report compiled the following year it was stated that 784 weapons were stored at Swanzey.

Henry Somerset had already been involved in serious fighting when, in April 1643, he visited Swanzey, presumably to boost morale in readiness for the king's summer offensive. The visit must have been brief, for the common attorneys' account records 'for my lord marquis of Worcester [and] his servants' diet and horse meat £10 9s. 4d.', and 19s. 2d. more was paid for one night's entertainment to Sir Marmaduke Lloyd, in all £11 8s. 6d.

The king had planned a threefold advance on London; as a preliminary it was deemed necessary to take Gloucester. The siege began in earnest when the Glamorgan militia, including the trained bands of Gower, advanced towards the city's west gate. Meanwhile, Walter Thomas had been ordered to raise a further 60 men from the Swanzey hundred as well as 20 men from the hundred of Llangyfelach and dispatch them to Cardiff. In a letter dated 13 August, Thomas complained that the order would impose hardship on the Swanzey hundred as 'their whole band is already in service', and pleaded for the Llangyfelach hundred to be spared. In a subsequent letter he stated that in the Swanzey hundred only 40 men could be impressed because the land had been 'so gleaned of all spare people ... of late that the husbandmen will hardly be able to manage their tillage [which would lead to] a scarcity of grain'. He also stated that the men were poorly armed, having 12 bill staves between them.

The king's advance ended when, on 20 September, his forces, which included the Glamorgan militia, were defeated at Newbury. News of the disaster would not have been received joyfully in Gower, nor would a demand for more money—Swanzey alone had to provide a hefty £120 16s. 8d. Hardly surprising, therefore, that whatever ill-will there may have been towards Puritan sympathizers was soon translated into religious persecution. On 26 July orders had been issued from Cardiff to the effect that the estates of all 'convicted separatists, fugitives and disaffected persons within' Gower were to be sequestrated, but no action appears to have been taken until, on 26 September, leading local officials took custody of the goods, lands and tenements of Rowland Dawkin and Ienkin Franklin of Ilston because they were 'persons disaffected to his majesty'. Both Dawkin and Franklin 'conformed' and were restored to their estates, but Dawkin subsequently left Gower to join the Parliamentary army.

In February 1644 Parliamentary forces under General Rowland Laugharne went on the offensive, moving out from their base in southern Pembrokeshire to overcome the Royalist strongholds in West Wales. By May, Laugharne's successes led to a Captain Robert Moulton, aboard the frigate *Lion* at Milford, writing a letter on behalf of others 'to the mayor and gentlemen of Swanzey', calling upon them to 'yield the town and garrison into the obedience of' Parliament and warning them that if they 'shall be obstinate and spill any blood in resisting', he would keep them 'without trade'. The reply, which was 'subscribed to by the high sheriff and most of the gentlemen of Glamorgan', began with the words: 'We cannot understand how we may … return you the name of gentlemen to your rude and rebellious paper', and concluded 'that we will neither yield town or garrison … but will defend the same and our county against your proud and insolent menacing'.

Moulton made good his threat, for it was later stated that 'parliamentary ships had taken many Swanzey boats and some of Cardiff'. Fortunately the town and garrison were saved from attack by the arrival in West Wales of Sir Charles Gerard, a ruthless Royalist commander, who quickly recaptured all that had been lost to Laugharne. It was while he lay siege to Pembroke in August that Gerard was recalled to deal with Parliamentarian attacks on the Welsh border.

With Gerard out of the way, and with reinforcements landed at Milford Haven, Laugharne went on the offensive again in November. Gerard duly returned to West Wales and defeated Laugharne at Newcastle Emlyn on 23 April 1645. To celebrate the victory the bells were rung at Swanzey, a hollow gesture because, in July, the men of south-east Wales were in a rebellious mood, fed up with the war, with Gerard's tyranny and with the king's repeated demands for men and money.

In June, Gerard had once again been recalled from West Wales to deal with trouble elsewhere, and once more Laugharne took the offensive, defeating Royalist forces on 1 August in a bloody battle at Colby Moor just outside Haverfordwest. On 12 October, Laugharne occupied Carmarthen, then advanced on Swanzey which he probably took without a fight because further east, beyond the Tawe, the situation

Rowland Laugharne

for the Royalists had deteriorated to the point where men were refusing to obey the king's instructions; those in the militia were calling themselves the 'Peaceable Army' and troops loyal to the king had been forced to leave Cardiff.

The common attorneys' account beginning Michaelmas 1645 records a payment of £1 0s. 4d. 'for wine and beer for entertainment of General Laugharne'. His stay may, therefore, have been short, but one of his priorities was to relieve Walter Thomas of his position as seneschal of Gower and governor of Swanzey and install Richard Donnell of Swanzey in his stead. On 17 November, Donnell was replaced on the instructions of Parliament by Colonel Philip Jones, then 27 years old. That same day, Bussy Mansel of Briton Ferry, a relative of the Mansels of Oxwich and Margam, and a former Royalist who had conveniently changed sides, was appointed commander-in-chief of all forces in Glamorgan.

While the war continued, Parliament was anxious that the most active Royalists should be removed from public office in favour of Parliamentary and Puritan sympathizers. An example of this occurred on 6 January 1646 when Walter Thomas and Leyson Seys of Swanzey were disenabled and debarred from serving as aldermen by a resolution of the town council—but if Parliament believed that such measures would frustrate a Royalist revival in Glamorgan, it was in for a rude surprise, for a dispatch dated 10 February 1646 mentions that Royalists were blockading Cardiff and were 'in possession of Swanzey'. There is clear evidence that, by 13 February dissident Royalists were laying siege to Cardiff Castle and continued to do so until, with the arrival of Laugharne five days later, they were compelled to withdraw.

Knowledge of what happened at Swanzey comes from an inquiry of 1650 in which persons unknown tried to discredit Philip Jones, claiming that, while he was governor of Swanzey, he allowed a troop of 38 horse under one Edward Gwynne to enter the town unopposed and seize the magazine, with the result that the rebels were able to send 'horse-loads thereof to the siege which they had laid before Cardiff'. In support of Jones, Colonel Rowland Dawkin refuted the charges, claiming that Jones had not been in the town when the magazine had been seized.

Another incident that took place at about this time, or shortly afterwards, involved William Thomas, son of Walter Thomas, who, with others, laid siege to Briton Ferry House, home of Bussy Mansel, the turncoat Royalist. The siege failed and on 25 February William Thomas voluntarily surrendered to Laugharne.

Walter Thomas compounded his delinquency—meaning he came to an agreement with Parliament—confessing that, 'being made governor of Swanzey, he did arm and array the inhabitants', presumably at the beginning of the war, although he could have been 'made governor' a second time during the 1646 rebellion. His fine was eventually fixed at £313. His son, William Thomas, also

Colonel Philip Jones

compounded, confessing that he had been appointed sheriff of Glamorgan at a time when Sir Charles Gerard had been campaigning in South Wales and had, therefore, been obliged to carry out his duties. He was certainly involved in an attempt to take Briton Ferry House during the February rebellion and his fine was fixed at £336.

At an unrecorded date in 1646, Henry Somerset died and his lands were confiscated by Parliament on account of his unswerving loyalty to the king. These events may have occurred early in the year because, on 7 May, Philip Jones obtained a 99-year lease on the forests of Llansamlet. The leasehold had been granted to him by Oliver Cromwell, which suggest either that Gower had already been confiscated by then, or that Cromwell—who may have had designs on the earl's estate—had sanctioned the lease as a personal favour to Jones.

It was in May, too, that the king gave himself up to the Scots. On 27 July the exiled minister, Ambrose Mostyn, returned to Gower to 'preach and officiate … in the parish church of Swanzey, as in the parishes ... adjacent' and continued to do so until he returned to North Wales in 1648.

While the king remained in Scotland, his supporters, though beaten, contemplated his return. There were Royalist spies everywhere, and one of them, writing from the Nag's Head in Goat Street, Swanzey, on 15 August 1646, informed the wife of an eminent Royalist that 'Colonel Jones went out of the town on Wednesday last. He did what he could in his business. I hear there are 100 horse to wait on Colonel [Bussy] Mansel and five companies [of infantry] are to remain in the garrisons of Cardiff and Swanzey'.

On 3 March 1647, Swanzey Castle was 'disgarrisoned and the works slighted' on the orders of Parliament. This must have entailed demolishing at least part of the curtain wall, possibly on the north and east as the west wall may have already been demolished to make way for the Townhall. In Oliver Cromwell's survey of 1650 the castle is described as 'An ancient decayed building called the new castle', and the survey also mentions 'a piece of ruinous building called the old castle'. Evidently, the site of the old castle had not been developed for tenements except for 'a little cottage adjoining'.

On 5 May the confiscated lands in Gloucestershire and Monmouthshire that had belonged to the marquis of Worcester were settled on Oliver Cromwell in recognition of his services during the war. At an unspecified date the same year Gower was also granted to Cromwell—not that he proved to be different from any other non-resident lord because the man who ruled Gower was still the seneschal. In Glamorgan as a whole, since the closing stage of the war, power had been in the hands of some 15 committeemen led by Philip Jones, his brother-in-law, John Price of Gellihir in the parish of Ilston, Rowland Dawkin and Bussy Mansel of Briton Ferry; the first three were undoubtedly Puritans, all were J.P.s.

In January 1648 General Rowland Laugharne was summoned to London to answer allegations that he had been conspiring with the king's agents. Parliament then gave orders for Laugharne's army to be disbanded, but Laugharne's associates refused to

Major-General Rowland Dawkin

comply with the orders, one of the events which precipitated the Second Civil War. In February, Laugharne's right-hand man, Colonel Rice Powell, marched eastwards and occupied Swanzey. In a later bid to discredit Jones it was stated, by persons unknown, that Powell, 'with a brace of pistols, singly forced Jones [and] his sentinels from their standings at Swanzey, he being then personally in the garrison and not making the least resistance, but permitted the said Powell to place sentinels of his own there … and so Jones quit the town and fled to Haverfordwest'.

In Jones's defence, Dawkin confirmed Powell's entry into Swanzey, stating that Powell had quartered two or three companies of foot in the town and posted his own sentinels, believing 'that it was unsafe for them to lay there unless they put a guard on their own men', but Dawkin denied that Jones had been in the town at the time of Powell's arrival.

Early in May, Powell marched into the Vale of Glamorgan to link up with die-hard Royalists. Meanwhile, Laugharne, who had made good his escape from London, passed through Swanzey, and the common attorneys' account records a payment of £4 'for grass that Major-general Laugharne [and] his troopers did make use of to Mr Walter Thomas'. On 4 May, Laugharne made contact with Powell in the vicinity of St. Fagans near Cardiff.

The man sent to deal with the rebels was Colonel Thomas Horton who positioned his troops to shield Cardiff. During the standoff that followed, Horton wrote to Cromwell on 6 May, saying that 'Colonel Philip Jones, with his company [of foot soldiers] from Swanzey … have been with us in all our march, and himself in many ways [has proved] helpful to us'. Early on 8 May, Horton was warned by scouts that the rebels were advancing on his position. The resulting Battle of St. Fagans raged for about two hours, but shortly after 10 a.m., Laugharne's forces were in full flight, heading westwards. In following up his victory Horton stopped at Swanzey, a fact confirmed by an entry in the common attorneys' account which states: 'Paid by Mr Portreeve, his order for the expense of 10 horses of Colonel Horton 15s.' Horton moved on in pursuit of Laugharne who had taken refuge in Pembroke Castle.

On 19 May, Cromwell himself arrived at Swanzey on his way to Pembroke. The Minute Book refers to him as 'lord of this town, the seigniory of Gower and manor of Kilvey' and mentions that he 'gave to the poor of this town to be set out at interest for the benefit and advantage of the said poor the sum of £10'. Pembroke Castle finally fell on 11 July after a 48-day siege, bringing the Second Civil War, as far as South Wales was concerned, to a close.

The Commonwealth

Charles 1's execution on 30 January 1649 marks the beginning of the Commonwealth; it also led to a rebellion in Ireland. That Cromwell stopped at Swanzey on his way to deal with the rebellion is confirmed by an entry, dated 2 September, in the Book of Common Hall, which records a payment of £10 to cover the cost of 'a dinner in the house of William Bayly, then Portreeve,' for Cromwell 'and for all his followers'. In the same entry the aldermen bemoan the fact that they 'were forced one night to entertain in the inns 40 horse [soldiers] with some foot on the public charge … amounting to £6 8s.' Reinforcements were soon following in Cromwell's footsteps, for in December 67 officers and men under the command of a Captain Nicholls were quartered in the town for five days at a cost of £2 3s. 4d. In March the following year 400,000 pounds of oatmeal were shipped to Ireland from Cardiff, Swanzey and Milford.

John Miles, a native of the Welsh-speaking part of Herefordshire, first came to Gower in 1641, but fled following the outbreak of war, possibly to become a chaplain in the New Model Army. When he returned to Gower in 1649 he established, at Ilston, the first Particular Baptist church in Wales. Between October that year and August 1660, 261 people joined his church, the majority of them women. He also established 'daughter' churches elsewhere, the most notable being at Hay, Llantrisant, Carmarthen and Abergavenny. Both Jones and Dawkin were members of his Ilston congregation and there can be no doubt that Miles owed his success to the support of these two powerful men.

Colonel Jones entered Parliament as a radical M.P. in February 1650 to give his support for the 'Act for the Propagation of the Gospel in Wales', the objective of which was to puritanize Wales and establish schools in which children could be taught in a Puritan atmosphere. In South Wales it fell to a commission headed by Jones, Dawkin, Price and Bussy Mansel to ensure that the work of propagation was carried out. The commission had powers to purge the Church of England of all undesirable ministers and replace them with men who upheld Puritan views. At least four ministers were ejected from their livings in Swanzey and Gower, the most notable being Hugh Gore, a native of Dorset, who was ejected from Oxwich and who made an alternative living for himself by setting up a school in Swanzey.

Among those to succeed to the livings of ejected ministers were Morris Bidwell, installed at St. Marys, Swanzey, and Marmaduke Matthew who, on his return from America, was installed in the chapel of St. Johns near Swanzey in 1655. That same year John ap John of Denbighshire, 'the Apostle of Quakerism in Wales', came to Swanzey where he made a few converts, one being William Bevan, a merchant who provided him with a site for a meeting house in the Strand. The Quakers soon made themselves unpopular in the town, being considered too outspoken in their views, too loud in their criticism, which they directed mainly at the Baptists. Throughout the late 1650s they suffered persecution in the form of abuse and imprisonment in the lower Townhall, and ministers of other denominations refused to bury them in their churchyards.

In 1650, Cromwell commissioned Bussy Mansel and John Price to carry out a survey of Gower, the objective of which was to record all that was due to Cromwell in the form of rents. The charter also makes it plain that, apart from Cromwell himself, the greatest landowner in Gower was Sir Edward Mansel who held the manors of Oxwich, Penrice, Port Eynon, Pitton and Pilton, Westown in Llangenydd,

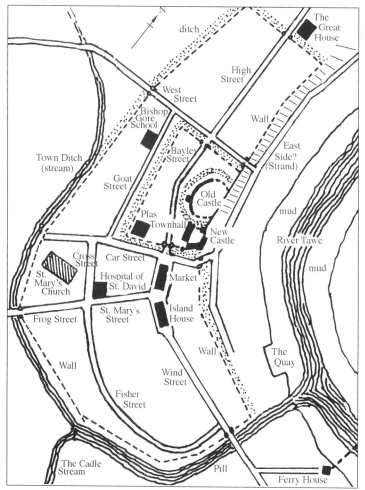

Map of Medieval Swansea

Stembridge, Llyn y bwch and Scurlage Castle, Walterston and Cilibion, *Brinavell* and Ilston, the Hospital of Swanzey and the manor or barony of Sketty. Bussy Mansel also appears in the survey as the owner of lands in the Llangyfelach hundred.

Also recorded are the number of tenements in Swanzey. Within the walls, Castle Bailey Street (which lay within the outer bailey and included the Plas) had 17 tenements, Wind Street had 39, West Side of the Market had 5, and may relate to the top end of Carstreet (now Caer Street) mentioned in 1656 as part of the Market Place, possibly the place where market traders parked their carts. Goat Street (which no longer exists, but ran a little to the east of what is now the upper part of Princess Way) had 38 tenements, Cross Street (between Goat Street and Fisher Street) had 11, Fisher Street (which curved eastwards from St. Mary's Church to the bottom end of Wind Street) had 12, East Side Within the Gates (possibly the east side of High Street, or one of the lanes leading to the Strand) had 8. West Street (now Collage Street) is not mentioned in the survey, but in 1400 it had 2½ burgages. St. Mary's Street had 26 tenements, Frog Street (formerly Streetend [?]; now the south side of St. Mary's Square) had 6. High Street Above the Gate had 17 tenements, East Side Without the Gate (probably the Strand) had 12, and Without the Gate (unlocated) had 7—in all 36 tenements lay outside the walls.

High Street Below the Gate, which in 1400 had 16 burgages, is mentioned in the survey, but the number of tenements is not given. What is mentioned is that

Philip Jones had 'A mansion house and garden in the High Street and adjoining the new dwelling house'. According to George Grant Francis in his *Charters Granted to the Chief Borough of Swanzey* of 1870, the new dwelling still existed in his day, and stood about 100m lower down than the house where Jones was born, next to the present-day Unitarian chapel in High Street; he described it as 'having oak panelling and carvings covering the walls of some of the rooms'. It is possible that the new building was where Jones attended to his affairs as alderman, seneschal of Gower, governor of Swanzey and Cardiff, comptroller of Cromwell's household, justice of the peace, Member of Parliament, chairman of the numerous committees that dealt with the religious, military and civil affairs of South Wales, to say nothing of the many properties he acquired during his years in power.

No mention is made of a market building in the survey, but by May 1651 the Corporation decided that £60 should be rated on the townspeople to defray the cost of a new covered market. A drawing of 1799 depicts the building as a large roof supported by 10 stone pillars, the floor area raised some 20cm. above a cobbled street. As to the lead that covered the roof, there is a tradition that during the siege of Pembroke in 1648 the lead, valued at £300, had been stolen from St. David's Cathedral or one of its chapels by Philip Jones.

Since 1648 South Wales had been governed by committeemen led by Philip Jones, Rowland Dawkin, Bussy Mansel and Jones's brother-in-law, John Price. When the first Protectorate Parliament sat in 1654, Jones was one of two men *selected* to represent Glamorgan while Price represented Cardiff. This gave Jones's critics a chance to go on the offensive, and on 30 August 1654 a commission was appointed to investigate the numerous allegations against Jones concerning his treatment of ejected clergymen and the misappropriation of sequested church lands. Jones could not have been more co-operative, first helping to draft the Act, then arranging for his own supporters to investigate the complaints. Unsurprisingly, the Propagation accounts were found to be in order.

Another example of Jones's influence occurred on 25 February 1655 (some sources argue in favour of 1656) when Cromwell presented Swanzey with a new charter. This charter was no gesture of goodwill, but part of Cromwell's nationwide policy to control troublesome borough officials, and there can be little doubt that Jones had a hand in its composition. Whilst confirming the burgesses in their time-honoured privileges, the charter stated that henceforth the town would be governed by a mayor (formally the portreeve), by a high seneschal (the first and only man to hold this title being Jones), a recorder (a man learned in the laws of England) and a common council made up of 12 aldermen and 12 capital burgesses. There could be only one free Guild of Merchants and the mayor, in conjunction with the common council, had the right to decide who could be a member of the guild and who could be a burgess, thereby abolishing the right to membership by birth, marriage or apprenticeship; they could also disfranchise any burgess whom they considered to be unsuitable. The first mayor, high seneschal and recorder were

The Townhall as it stood in 1820. It was built before 1640 and remained in use until the Guildhall on the Little Burrows was completed in 1829

all republicans; so, too, were the majority of aldermen (the most important being Rowland Dawkin who took the place of Jones) and capital burgesses (one being John Price). The Townhall was renamed the Guildhall.

The charter outlined the boundaries of the borough (later known as the Town and Franchise of Swanzey) which, although more detailed, corresponded to the boundaries mentioned in Earl William's 12th-century charter. The new charter also provides a list of council officers—the town clerk/clerk of the peace, two serjeants-at-mace (whose duties were serving notices and executing warrants), two chamber-lains (formally the common attorneys), two head constables and one water bailiff (the executive officer of the port).

The high point in Rowland Dawkin's career came when an insurrection in Wiltshire in March 1655 led to the rule of the major-generals. In October the realm was divided into 11 military districts. Gower and, indeed, the whole of South Wales were placed temporarily under the command of two men, one being Major-General Dawkin. By the summer of 1656, Dawkin had his command reduced, being appointed deputy major-general of Glamorgan. Rule by army officers proved to be extremely unpopular due to their ban on various forms of entertainment and their insistence on a strict observance of the Sabbath.

Army rule ended early in 1657, and in June that year, Cromwell accepted the proposal for an 'Other House' to take the place of the House of Lords, which comprised of 40 picked members, one of whom proved to be Philip Jones. There were changes in the composition of the House of Commons too. On 3 May 1658,

Cromwell granted Swanzey another charter whereby 'there shall be within the said town and borough ... one Burgess of the Parliament'. This charter was an attempt by Cromwell to secure a compliant Parliament because there appears to be no record of an election.

Cromwell died on 3 September 1658, his lavish funeral arrangements being superintended by Jones, to be succeeded as Protector by his son, Richard. The Swanzey Corporation celebrated Richard's succession by having the bells rung and spending 16s. 10d. on gunpowder and match, presumably for guns to be fired. When Richard called a Parliament for 27 January 1659 the man to represent Swanzey was William Foxwist of Caernafon, a Welsh circuit judge loyal to Cromwell, whose seat in the House of Commons is likely to have been secured by Jones. When the irregularity of Foxwist's return was raised in the House it was proposed there should be an inquiry into the affair. The Parliament lasted only three months, time enough for certain M.P.s to renew their attack on Jones over the huge sums of money that had gone missing from the Propagation fund, but events intervened. Richard could not command the respect of the army as his father had done, and on 22 April the generals forced him to dissolve Parliament. There followed a year of political uncertainly as one Parliament succeeded another.

In May two pamphlets appeared, one condemning Jones as a coward and drawing attention to how, in ten years, he had multiplied his yearly earnings from £50 to £5,000 (the true figure being little more than £1,000). The other pamphlet stated that Jones had 'recommended, nominated and brought into authority [in South Wales] divers notorious cavaliers in arms, compounded delinquents and disaffected persons'. Jones answered his critics before the restored 'Rump' Parliament on 23 May, denying all charges, and subsequently thwarted attempts to have him charged for bribing witnesses—but the damage done to his character forced him to temporarily retire from politics and forfeit his governorship of Cardiff Castle. Things were not going well for Jones's principle associates either, for it was about this time that Dawkin, who had already lost his seat for Carmarthen the previous year, was relieved of his governorship of Tenby. John Price was also deprived of positions of authority, whereas Bussy Mansel appears to have been favoured by the opposition to the extent that he became a leading committeeman of Glamorgan.

Elections were called for April 1660 to prepare for the restoration of the monarchy. Sir Edward Mansel was one of two men to be returned for Glamorgan, whilst his cousin, Bussy Mansel, was elected member for Cardiff (taking the place of John Price) and the six associated boroughs, including Loughor and Swanzey, which no longer returned an M.P. of its own.

In view of the changing political situation the Swanzey Corporation set aside Cromwell's charter, reverting to the way things had been prior to its enactment. At Michaelmas 1659 the title of mayor was dropped in favour of portreeve. The final *volte face* took place the following year when Charles II was recalled from exile. On

11 May the Corporation spent £4 7s. to entertain Jones's arch-adversary, Colonel Edward Freeman, in the house of Lyson Seys. That same day a proclamation was read concerning the return of 'his Most Gracious Majesty, Charles II, to be king'. The town went wild with bells ringing, bonfires blazing and the dispensation of beer. There is no evidence that Jones took part in the celebration.

CHAPTER VIII
From the Restoration to the early 18th century

Following the restoration of Charles II, Gower was restored to Henry Somerset, third marquis of Worcester. Somerset's agents arrived in Swanzey sometime after Michaelmas 1660, for the common attorneys' account for the year 1660-61 records a payment 'for the marquis of Worcester's commissioners £1 9s. 8d; for a loaf of refined sugar 6s; and for their horse meat £1 15s. 6d'. The account for that same year also records 7s. 6d. 'for cutting the portcullis on the town seal', symbolizing a return to former customs and practices.

Before his arrival in England, Charles had promised 'a liberty for tender consciences' in the hope that it would lead to religious tolerance—for Catholics as well as Puritans—but the 'Cavalier' Parliament of 1661 had no intention of allowing the Puritans to retain their positions of power. In December that year Parliament passed a Bill for Regulating the Corporations, the intention of which was to control the boroughs, and thereby Parliament itself as the burgesses were responsible for electing many M.Ps. In future all borough officials were to take an oath of allegiance and non-resistance to the king, promising to take the sacraments according to rites of the Church of England. In Swanzey two men, one of them Rowland Dawkin, were relieved of their aldermanic status, presumably because they refused to take the oath, to be replaced by two Royalists—Leyson Seys and William Thomas.

Beyond the town the Baptists at Ilston were among the first to suffer a reversal of fortune in that, on 23 July 1660, instructions were issued for their pastor, John Miles, to be replaced by the Anglican minister, William Houghton, who had himself been relieved of his living of Penmaen before the Civil War. There is a tradition that Miles and his congregation built a new church at Trinity Well in the secluded Ilston Valley, a view supported by the fact that Rowland Dawkin owned the land, although there are those who would argue that Trinity Well may have been founded by William Houghton. Whatever the truth, the treatment of Baptists was nothing compared to that meted out to the Quakers, for later that year the portreeve, Leyson Seys, accompanied by officers armed with halberds, broke up a Quaker gathering in the town and imprisoned all the men.

Ignoring the king's wish for tolerance, Parliament passed the Act of Uniformity on 16 May 1662, requiring that all ministers followed the guidelines laid down in the Anglican Book of Common Prayer. This proved unacceptable to men such as Marmaduke Matthew, causing him to give up his living at St. Johns. Nor was the requirement acceptable to John Miles, and in 1663 he sailed to America with about 15 of his flock where he joined with other Baptists to found a settlement in Massachusetts, which he called Swanzey. The settlement was attacked by Indians in 1675 when the church and a number of buildings were burnt. Miles died in 1683. The records of his Ilston and Swanzey congregations are preserved in the library on Rhode Island.

Between 1662-68, about 100 laymen in Gower were hauled before the consistory court at Carmarthen for refusing to attend services at Anglican churches, among them Philip Jones and Rowland Dawkin. Eventually Jones conformed, but Dawkin remained a Nonconformist to the very end. Both men had enemies in high places, but Jones appears to have had the respect of Royalists in Swanzey and Glamorgan, his place among the leading gentry accepted despite the fact that his many estates, including Fonmon Castle in the Vale, had come into his possession as a result of private purchase during the Commonwealth period. Dawkin, too, appears to have been respected both as a soldier and for the strength of his religious convictions.

In 1664 Parliament passed the Conventicle Act, prohibiting religious gatherings of five people or more that were not in accordance with the Common Prayer Book. Punishment ranged from fines and/or imprisonment to transportation for seven years. Marmaduke Matthew was accused of keeping conventicles on three separate occasions, yet he seems to have escaped transportation. Indeed, it was said of him that he continued to preach 'at a little chapel at the end of town by the connivance of the magistrates'. Reluctance on the part of the civil authorities to take action against those who dissented is borne out by a letter, written by Bishop Lucy of St. Davids, which calls upon men of authority to deal with the Dissenters who met at two farms near Llangyfelach Church, whom he described as 'dangerous … and an affront to the established religion'.

On 15 March 1672, Charles II proclaimed his Declaration of Indulgence whereby the penal laws against Dissenters were suspended. There were still restrictions, however, in that Dissenters could only worship in approved places under licensed preachers. One of the first men in Gower to take advantage of the new conditions was Marmaduke Matthew who, on 12 April, obtained a licence to preach in his home in Swanzey, which became a meeting house for the Independents. The fortunes of the Dissenters fluctuated over the next few years, but in the returns made to the archbishop of Canterbury in 1676 it was recorded that there were 292 adult Dissenters in Swanzey and as many as 400 in Gower as whole. There is reason to believe that these figures are well below the true totals.

Thirty-one years after the 'new' castle had been disgarrisoned a Yorkshireman, Francis Place, created a pen and wash drawing of Swanzey as it appeared to him

Francis Place's pen and wash drawing of Swanzey from the east bank of the Tawe in 1678

from the east bank of the River Tawe. The drawing is remarkable in that it is the earliest surviving view of the town. It depicts the ruins of the 'new' castle and, further north, a small tower with a pyramid-shaped roof; between the castle and the small tower is a length of wall, evidence that the eastern wall of the 'old' castle still existed in 1678. A later drawing, dated 1729, shows that part of the eastern wall had been removed, which suggests that by then the burgesses were no longer concerned with defence.

In the 1678 drawing Francis Place scrawled the words 'glas house' above the north-east tower of the 'new' castle. A deed of 1684 records that a Robert Wilmott of Gloucester took out a seven-year lease on the tower which he and his partner, John Man of Swanzey, had converted into a glass house for making bottles. Two years later Wilmott sold the lease to Man who promised, as part payment, to supply Wilmott with 5,040 bottles. The glass works still existed in 1696.

Hugh Gore, as bishop of Waterford and Lismore in Ireland, returned to Swanzey in 1682 and, out of 'the love he bore to the ... borough ... and to the burgesses and inhabitants thereof', made arrangements in September to establish a free grammar school for the benefit of '20 poor children and youths, sons of the poorer sort of burgesses', to be instructed 'in the Latin and Greek tongues'. The school, built in Goat Street on land belonging to Bussy Mansel, had a history of neglect, but the present-day Bishop Gore School in Sketty serves as a reminder of the man and his good intentions.

Henry Somerset, third marquis of Worcester, had been Lord President of the Council in the Marches of Wales for ten years when, in November 1682, he became the first duke of Beaufort. As Lord President he made an almost regal progress through the principality in 1684, arriving at Swanzey to be 'met and complimented by the gentlemen of this county', according to his historiographer, Thomas Dineley,[1] and 'was conducted by them to the lodgings prepared for him, where he found an ample entertainment ... The next morning, August 16, his Grace ... went on foot to morning prayer at St. Mary's Church', after which he 'took a view of the town and harbour, some part of which was beautified for his reception'.

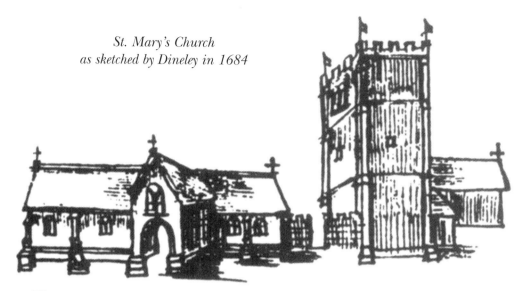

St. Mary's Church
as sketched by Dineley in 1684

The purpose of the duke's progress was essentially to review borough charters on behalf of the king. Swanzey was obliged to surrender its existing charter in return for a new one, dated 28 March 1685, issued in the name of King James II. In many respects the new charter was similar to Cromwell's, the title of portreeve being replaced by that of mayor. The charter named Sir Edward Mansel as the man selected to be the first mayor. There were to be 12 aldermen, including the mayor, deputy-mayor and the steward, William Herbert. These changes were intended to give the king, through Mansel, Herbert and others, more control over the borough, the appointment of borough officials, the selection of new burgesses and the removal of anyone found to be unsuitable. Although the charter raised the number of capital burgesses from 12 to 15 it tended to limit the number of new burgesses, making the corporate body more manageable. For reasons that are unclear this charter does not appear to have been implemented; moreover, the chief burgess continued to be called the portreeve, and the man who held that title without interruption between Michaelmas 1678 and Michaelmas 1688 was Thomas Phillips.

James II issued his own Declaration of Liberties in 1687, similar to the one issued by his brother, Charles II, in 1672. Then, in 1689, William of Orange and his wife, Mary, implemented their Toleration Act, allowing Dissenters more freedom than they had known for almost 30 years. The Presbyterians of Swanzey were not slow in taking advantage of the Act, for that same year they built the town's first chapel, which soon proved to be too small for their growing congregation. In 1698 they built a large chapel in High Street on the site of the present-day Unitarian church. The Baptists rented the smaller chapel, later known as the Old Meeting House, which stood at the top of Orchard Street in what became Baptist Court.

Edward Lhuyd published his survey of Wales in 1696, recording what his correspondent, Isaac Hamon, had to say about the people on the 'south side' of the peninsula speaking Old English, and those on the 'north side' inclining more to the Welsh. Swanzey and Loughor were undoubtedly bilingual, but in the Welshry the native language persisted. Irrespective of their racial origin it has been estimated that about this time more than three-quarters of the population were dependant primarily on agriculture, yet farm labourers appear to have been relatively few, fewer perhaps than domestic servants. By far the majority of those who worked the land were tenant farmers, holding their farms on a variety of tenures, either for a specified number of years, or for up to three lives, and there were still many customary tenants whose rents appear small, but who were subject to the payment of fines and heriots and who were obliged to carry out labour dues to their lord.

In the upland hundred of Llangyfelach the emphasis was, as in earlier centuries, on flocks and herds—dairy cattle, small sheep and goats. Oats was the main crop with small quantities of wheat and barley grown in the narrow valleys. In the Swansea Hundred mixed farming predominated. Oats was still the most extensive crop here, but its use may have been for fodder rather than bread. Wheat and barley were important, as were peas and beans, but there seems to have been only a limited requirement for hay. As with the uplands, dairy and store cattle (for meat) were the most valuable stock, 'reds' and 'blacks' being the most frequently mentioned breeds in surviving wills. Sheep were as versatile as ever, the native breed being a Down sheep. Horses were indispensable for farm work, several of which were present on even the smaller farms. Pigs were more common here than in the uplands, as were bees and rabbits.

For farm labourers, tenant and yeoman farmers, working the land was to a large extent seasonal work—July, August and September being the busiest months. During the winter whole families, including the men, gathered together to card and spin wool, then knit socks which they sold at local fairs. Near the coast the peasantry

Typical of the limekilns that still dot the peninsula, this example is above Tor Bay, Penmaen

collected seaweed which they burnt, transforming it into kelp, then selling it for use in the manufacture of glass bottles, as at Swanzey Castle. Kelp was also required by men such as Griffith Jenkins who, in 1690, produced soap in his 'soap house' in Swanzey. However, most of the kelp was transported to Bristol.

Cromwell's survey of 1650 refers to the 'custom of [tenant farmers in] the said lordship, time out of mind', of digging and breaking up 'all manner of stone at their pleasure', most of it limestone which they burnt in limekilns for use as fertilizer. The limekilns that still dot the peninsula are testimony to this activity. From about 1600 onwards increasing quantities of limestone were shipped to Devon to such an extent that the coastline of the peninsula—from Mumbles to Rhosili—became littered with limestone rubble and has remained so till the present day. Hundreds of small boats arrived during the summer months, discharging their ballast upon the beaches to form huge mounds of stones which were augmented by limestone rubble, the most impressive being those that have survived at Pwlldu Bay. By the 19th century, quarrying offered full-time employment with stockpiling taking place during the winter months. Boats were loaded at ebb tide, the women raising the stones to their knees, the men lifting the stones over the gunwales. It must have been thirsty work because, at one time, there were two public houses in the now tranquil Pwlldu Bay, where quarrying ceased in the second decade of the 20th century.

Men were also required to fell trees for ship-building, for pit props and, in the early part of the 18th century, to produce charcoal for the iron industry which

Pwlldu Bay—tranquil now, but the huge piles of smooth grey stones bear testimony to the extensive quarrying that went on here until it ceased in the early 20th century, when commercial fertilizers superseded burnt lime

required an acre of woodland to produce one ton of iron. The iron works of note were the Forest forge, Landore (erected in 1697), Ynyscedwyn (in operation by 1717) and Ynyspenllwch, near Clydach (in operation before 1750). Additional or alternative employment could be found in coalmining, especially during the winter months when demand was at its highest, even for the small-time farmers who, with their horses, were employed to transport coal from the mines to the nearest river-side quays. The dirt and danger of coalmining did not deter men from working underground. In the early 18th century the daily wage of a farm worker was 6d., whereas a collier's daily wage was 10d., enough to attract seasonal workers from all over South Wales and from across the Bristol Channel. Coal also attracted industri-alists who would, one day, make Swanzey the copper metropolis of the world.

As to those who were not primarily dependent on the land (less than 25% of the population), they largely fell into two groups. There were those whose occupa-tions stemmed from agriculture (such as millers, butchers, brewers and tanners) and those who were craftsmen unconnected with agricultural produce (such as blacksmiths, sail makers and carpenters). Only a small proportion of the populace earned their living primarily as colliers, sailors, shopkeepers and the like, but their numbers were to increase in the succeeding centuries.

Politically, the Act of Union had linked Gower to Cardiff and the former lord-ship of Glamorgan, but due to the difficulties of travelling overland Gower's economic ties were mainly with Bristol and the West Country; they were to remain so for a variety of reasons until the end of the 19th century. The shipping of raw material such as limestone, coal and copper, of livestock and dairy products from places such as Port Eynon to Bristol, and the purchase of a variety of luxury goods and hardware from that same city led to continued settlement of Gower by West Country sailors, entrepreneurs and industrialists until, by the early 19th century, workers in industry drawn from across the Bristol Channel almost rivalled the numbers of workers from all parts of South Wales.

One of the most notable men from Cornwall was Dr. John Lane who, in 1717, took out a lease on 'the other old copper works at Landore', the old furnaces being removed and replaced by 20 new ones. Lane knew all about copper: he shared a partnership in Cornish copper mines; he knew, too, that it took an estimated 18 tons of coal to produce one ton of copper. It was, therefore, easier to ship the copper ore to where coal could be mined in abundance. There was no shortage of mines in and around Landore, and the copper works—known as the Llangyfelach Works—occupied the low ground north of what later became known as the Landore viaduct. The works had been sited close to the River Tawe where 60-ton ships could offload ore onto quays and return to Cornwall with cargoes of coal. Lane was fortu-nate in his choice of manager, a Shropshire man named Robert Morris, who made the venture profitable. In 1720-23 a second copper works, the Cambrian, was estab-lished by a group of Quakers outside the town walls, on the low ground below High Street Station. By the end of the century another five copper works had come into being near the Tawe, four of them on the east bank between Llansamlet and Foxhole; there were also copper works at Penclawdd and Loughor. By 1800 the copper ore came not only from Cornwall, but also, though in smaller quantities, from Anglesey and Ireland.

The main reason for the early industrialization of the Tawe and Neath valleys and, to a lesser extent, the Loughor estuary, was the availability of coal in close proximity to the sea. The coal still had to be transported by packhorse to the riverside quays, but the distance was relatively short, whereas, further east, the distance and difficult terrain between the coal-rich valleys and the sea denied ports such as Cardiff the benefits associated with coal until the promotion of canals in the 1890s. When Daniel Defoe visited Swanzey in 1722 he wrote, in his *Tour Through England and Wales*, that Swanzey was a 'sea-port, and a very great trade for coal and culm [anthracite coal dust] which they export to all parts of Somerset, Devon and Cornwall and also to Ireland itself; so that one sometimes sees a hundred sail of ships at a time loading coals here, which greatly enriches' the town. The following year it was estimated that 80% of the coal shipped from Swanzey was carried in ships that brought in the copper ore. No one epitomizes the coal owners of the 18th century more than Chauncey Townsend, a London merchant who came to Swanzey to invest in the coal trade. According to a great-grandson, the collieries 'at Llansamlet [and Birchgrove] were originally opened by the said Chauncey Townsend about the year 1750'. Townsend constructed what may have been Gower's first tramway, which enabled horse-drawn wagons to convey coal from

Scott's Pit Engine House, Birchgrove, built by Captain John Scott between 1816 and 1819 for pumping water from what was then the Old Church Colliery. From this colliery to the Foxhole quays, Scott built a railway line—one of the oldest in Wales. The line was incorporated into the Swansea Vale Railway in 1845

his Llansamlet/Birchgrove collieries to the quays at Foxhole. After his death in 1770, Townsend's collieries remained part of a family concern, and by 1841 they provided work for 421 men, producing about 70,000 tons of coal per year.

By 1738 the Anglican Church had fallen 'asleep' and the Dissenters were given to disputation among themselves. When the Anglican revivalist (Methodist), Howell Harris, arrived in Gower late that year his fiery sermons on the assurance of salvation appealed to Anglicans and Dissenters alike. Many left the Anglican Church to become Methodists and many Dissenters joined them. Within ten years there were a dozen Methodist societies in the Welsh-speaking areas of Gower.

Associated with the Methodist revival were the circulating schools of Griffith Jones, a Carmarthenshire rector. In 1738, Jones began dispatching itinerant teachers all over South Wales to teach poor children in the day and adults in the evening to read the Bible, the Common Prayer Book and instruct them in the catechism—in English and Welsh depending on what language prevailed in any given locality. All the Gower parishes, including Swanzey, were to benefit from Jones's teachers. Schooling took place during the winter months in churches, farms and cottages. Following Jones's death in 1761 his work was carried on by Madam Bevan of Laugharne until 1771.

It was bad enough that St. Mary's Church was seriously damaged in 1704, but in 1739, while extensive repairs were being carried out, the roof of the nave collapsed. It had been customary for the congregation to wait outside until the arrival of the vicar; fortunately on this occasion he turned up late, for had he been on time a great many people would have been killed. The church, however, was rebuilt under the supervision of Thomas Woodward of Worcester.

Samuel and Nathaniel Buck published their copper engraving entitled 'The East View of Swanzey Castle' in 1741. The south block of the 'new' castle dominates the engraving. To the right is a gap in the curtain wall through which the roof of

The Bucks' 'East View of Swanzey Castle' of 1741

the Townhall can be seen; the ruinous building to the right is the north-eastern tower of the 'new' castle. In 1742 a Swanzey mercer, Leyson Morgan, took out a lease on 'all that Castle of Swanzey', presumably for storing his wares. Looking further to the right there appears to be a tree-lined mound with a bench close to the trees. The mound has been interpreted as the remains of the 12th-century motte, although there are those who would argue that the mound is an exaggeration of the lie of the land. Further to the right is a walled enclosure with a corner tower having a pyramid-like roof. Although they appear to be in a good state of repair, the tower and the embattled part of the wall are the remains of the 'old' castle. The tree-lined mound—and possibly the walled enclosure as well—are referred to in Cromwell's charter as 'Two little gardens adjoining to the house of the said Walter [Thomas] called the Old Castle Gardens'. In 1762 George Venables Vernon held the lease on 'those two gardens called the Castle Gardens and the summer house'. The summer house may have been the corner tower, in which case one of the 'little gardens' must have lain within the adjoining walls. In September 1750 a lease was obtained for the south block of the 'new' castle for the purpose of converting it into a poor house, or workhouse, in the charge of the churchwardens and overseers of the poor. The south block remained a workhouse until 1817.

The Mansel family of Oxwich and Margam expired in the male line in 1750, the huge family estate passing to Mary Mansel and her husband, John Ivory Talbot of Lacock Abbey. In 1768 the estate passed to Mary's grandson, Thomas Mansel Talbot, who, between 1773-79, built a four-storeyed mansion —known as Penrice Castle— near the 14th-century castle that had belonged to the Penreses. This was no mean feat as the building materials had to be shipped to Oxwich and transported overland through woods and marshes. In his *Two Successive Tours Throughout the whole of Wales*, published in 1798, Henry Skrine questioned what 'disposed Mr Talbot to create

Thomas Rothwell's engraving of Penrice Castle in 1792

Briton Ferry and Vernon House as engraved by Thomas Rothwell in 1792

a highly ornamented villa, with all its luxurious appendages at Penrice', although he did concede that 'the house is an elegant modern structure, and the diversities of lawn, wood and water, introduced with much taste and design', contrasted with 'the surrounding district', but seemingly disapproved of 'the principle approach through fictitious fragments of a modern ruin', which today deceive passing motorists into thinking that they are part of a ruined castle.

1750 was also the year in which the huge estate of the Briton Ferry branch of the Mansel family passed to Barbara Mansel who, in 1751, married a Derbyshire man, George Venables Vernon.

The first lead works was established at Middle Bank on the east bank of the Tawe in 1755, and in 1757 a second lead works was established close by at Upper Bank, which also produced spelter—impure zinc.

During the 1750s several Gower shipbuilders applied to the Admiralty for protection against impressment for their key workers: Leyson Bowen of Mumbles secured protection for eight shipwrights; Paul Bevan obtained similar privileges for his eight sailmakers. Protection certificates were necessary because there were press gangs active in Swanzey with orders to impress anyone 'who used the sea' and were not in possession of a protection certificate. One of the most infamous press gangs operating in Swanzey and Gower at that time was the 13-man crew of a cutter named the *Caesar*, a merchantman under the command of a naval lieutenant, James Gaborian. These insensitive ruffians are known to have carried out a brutal attack on two Gower men in the vicinity of Brynmill, the incident being well documented. On 28 November 1760 the *Caesar* left the shelter of Mumbles Head with a cargo of over 50 impressed men. Late in the afternoon the cutter ran into a storm and was driven onto the rocks at Pwlldu Head. Lieutenant Gaborian made it to safety, as did two of the crew, but according to the Admiralty 65 men and three women lost their lives, most of them trapped beneath battened down hatches. According to the locals 97 bodies were buried in a mass grave on Pwlldu Head, the covering mound of which is still known as Gravesend.

The Plas had been neglected for many years prior to the death of Thomas Herbert. The death of his wife and child the following year initiated a 20-year legal battle for the Herbert estate, this eventually being settled on two sisters, one of whom inherited the Herbert properties in Gower and, in 1763, her husband, Calvert Richard Jones, repaired the Plas and took up residence there, allowing the Methodist, John Wesley, to preach in his 'green courtyard'. Jones's son and name-sake resided at the Plas until about 1800, after which it fell into disrepair again. Then, in 1840, John Henry Vivian purchased the ruins, removing some of the jambs, mullions, transoms and windows to install them in his home farm at Singleton—features which today can be seen in the house adjoining the Oystermouth Road entrance to Singleton Park.

The earliest recorded pottery works, the Cambrian, was established in 1764 on the site of the defunct copper works of that name. The clay came mainly from the

Home farm of the Vivians. The stone windows and other details were taken from The Plas in 1840

west of England and the finished products are said to be on a par with those of Wedgwood; they were certainly good enough for Lord Nelson to purchase several items during his visit to the works in 1802. The pottery passed into the hands of the Dillwyn family in 1801-02, which led to the famous Dillwyn's Etruscan Ware in 1847. A rival, the Glamorgan Pottery, began production in 1813 and, between them, the two potteries employed over 400 people until, in 1848-49, the Dillwyns took over the rival works and closed it down. Three other potteries were in operation in the late 19th century.

Prior to the Turnpike Act of 1764 the highways and byways in Gower were in a deplorable state, little more than mire and stones, often flooded. The main highway from Neath ran through Coed Franc to Abertawe where travellers had to risk wading across the bay when the tide was out, or make use of the ferry—either way they risked being swamped by freshets and there were lengthy delays caused by the tide and passing ships. Beyond the town the highways were 'long lines of barren, desolate, uninhabited tracks'. Travellers could ride or walk, but their goods, if they were heavy, had to be conveyed by packhorses. The Act of 1764 apportioned Glamorgan into five trusts, Swanzey being one, with powers 'to raise capital ... by gates and toll-bars for ... improving' the main highways through Gower. The gentry took up the challenge, arranging for ditches to be dug, vegetation to be cut back and the road surfaces to be improved. The Strand appears to have been their first priority, which they straightened and made a turnpike road in 1765. Their most notable achievement was to improve what remains the main route through Gower— now taken by the M4 motorway. It ran from Neath, passing Llansamlet Church 'over the fields to and over Forrest Bridge' above Morriston; from there improved highways led to Loughor, Pontardulais and Penlle'r Castell on the northern border.

Following the death of his father (Robert Morris) in 1768, Sir John Morris look his place in the Morris, Lockwood Company to become one of the leading industrialists of his day, having charge of copper smelting works at Landore and at Forest near Morriston, as well as numerous collieries in both localities. It was probably Sir John, rather than his father, who built the 'lofty mansion' of Clasemont on the hill above Morriston. According to one source, he 'seems to have been the

Morris Castle—the remains of a block of flats built by John Morris in the 18th century, designed to house 40 colliers and their families

The Forest Copper Works at Morriston, as engraved by Thomas Rothwell in 1791

most extensive individual builder of habitations for the labouring class. He first erected a kind of castellated lofty mansion … containing dwellings for 40 families, all colliers, excepting one tailor and one shoemaker, who are considered useful appendages'. The remains of this castle-like mansion can be seen on the high ground above Cwm Level Road. It is possibly one of the first block of flats ever built in this country. 'About the year 1768 he laid the foundations of Morriston [which was named after him] where dwellings have been erected for colliers and manufacturers in well formed and spacious streets: with a church [St. John's Anglican Church founded in 1795] containing an organ for such of his workmen as preferred the established religion … he erected also a chapel for non-conformists [Libanus in 1782] … in 1796 there were 141 houses inhabited by 619 persons'. Although the Tawe was navigable as far as the Beaufort Bridge below Morriston on normal tides, Sir John involved himself in a joint venture to construct a canal from the coal banks at Landore to his Forest Works near Morriston about a mile away. The canal was just over a mile in length and seems to have been completed about 1790. Sir John died in 1818; his successors continued to be men of wealth and influence into the 20th century.

The 1770s saw a number of changes. Swanzey's first bank, the Glamorgan and Swanzey Bank, opened in Wind Street in 1771. In 1777 the first zinc spelter works was established at Middle Bank on the east side of the Tawe, opposite the Hafod. The Wych Tree Bridge Trust came into existence in 1778, having powers to build a new bridge at Morriston; seven years later the main road into Carmarthenshire crossed the Loughor at Pontardulais.

Between 1770 and 1788 the burgesses of Swanzey rarely met in the Common Hall, for they were the years when the word of Gabriel Powell, the seneschal, 'was law'. For several years, Powell refused to allow the 'ruinous condition' of the streets to be rectified, he disapproved of promoting the town as a resort, and blocked all attempts to obtain an Act of Parliament for the improvement of the harbour to the extent that, in a meeting held on 2 November 1787, his total disregard for opposing views led to a brawl between his son, the Revd. Thomas Powell, and one of the petitioners. So how did this irascible old man earn the name of 'King of Swanzey'? He did not have the power of life and death as George Herbert had had 200 years earlier, but he still had the last word as to who could be portreeve, or even a burgess, thereby excluding anyone whom he considered to be confrontational. He restricted the number of burgesses to the extent that by the time of his death there were only 35 of them. As to those burgesses, they had no sense of communal responsibility, but saw themselves as a privileged class and considered Powell to be one of them as, indeed, he was, having held the position of portreeve in 1740. After his death in December 1788 the Corporation met on 23 occasions the following year and, without his influence, even went so far, in October, as to order the construction of bathing machines 'on the pattern of those ... at Weymouth'. In December the Corporation voted to spend £300 on purchasing and improving a large premises at St. Helens for use as a bathing house; two years later the Swanzey Harbour Act was obtained. Unfortunately, it was not until the establishment of the Paving and Lighting Commission in 1809 that the Corporation became increasingly involved in public administration.

Until 1774 people still used Cromwell's market; they also made use of Island House which the Revd. John Oldisworth, in his *Swanzey Guide* of 1802, described as 'on the south side of Market Square ... which was still used both by butchers and local farmers. Round three sides of the northern portion of Island House was a kind of verandah, with wooden pillars and a copper roof, under which were fixed a line of hooks'. Island House was part of the 'shambles' where butchers sold their wares. A lease was obtained from the duke of Beaufort in 1774 for the 'new' castle court-yard and a plot of land immediately to the north to be used as the site of a new market, consisting of a penthouse roof around the perimeter, the central area open to the elements. Unfortunately, this market was a failure, the butchers boycotting it because the Corporation refused to compensate them for the loss of their established stalls. The new meat market was not entirely unused, for in 1816 it was reported to have been occupied by those who sold poultry, butter and a few sheep.

The Cromwellian market at the top of Wind Street as depicted by John Nixon in 1799. Note the cobbled street and the 'new' castle garderobe tower beyond the rooftops. Even when a new market was built in 1774 within the castle precincts the Cromwellian market continued in use until its demolition in 1822

During the late 18th century the first floor of the north-east tower of the 'new' castle was converted into a debtors' prison. This entailed rebuilding the west wall and covering the four rooms on the first floor with a roof. The prison could accommodate ten inmates, each of whom had to provide his own food, fuel and furniture. The administration caused 'surprise' to at least one observer, who noted that one inmate was able to ply his trade as a book-binder in order to pay off his debts. The prison, which had belonged to the dukes of Beaufort, closed in 1858 as a result of an Act of Parliament which proclaimed that all debtors should be placed in the Queen's prisons.

Twenty years after the Turnpike Act of 1768 the main highways through South Wales must have improved considerably, for on 28 August 1788 the *Bristol Gazette* announced that the *Diligence* would depart from the Mackworth Arms (on the site of the later G.P.O.) in Wind Street, Swanzey, at 4 a.m. every Sunday, Wednesday and Friday to arrive the same evening at the New Passage, where a boat would take passengers over the Severn, and that a coach would be waiting for them at 8 a.m. the following morning to convey them to Bristol; the fare 30s. A further 23 years

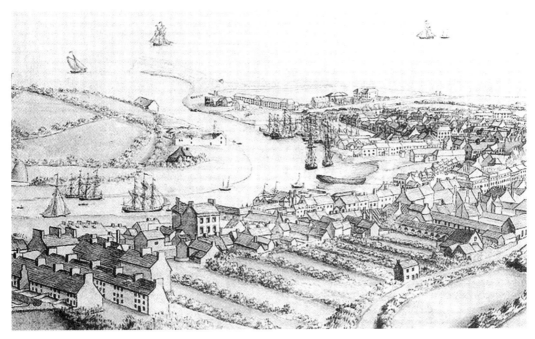

Paul Padley's view of Swansea from the north-west

later the London *Times* declared, on 10 September 1811, that Spencer's coaches were the only day-time carriages travelling from London to South Wales, the journey via Ross-on-Wye taking two days.

An act of 1791 led to the creation of the Swanzey Harbour Trust, the money raised being used for the construction of a lighthouse on Mumbles Head, which initially consisted of two coal lights, one above the other and separated by a height of 6m; it had 'to be kept constantly burning throughout' the night 'for the benefit and security of ships' passing Mumbles Head. The Act also led to the construction of two breakwaters to enclose Fabian's Bay. In his *Letters Written During A Tour Through South Wales, in the year 1803*, the Revd. J. Evans wrote 'Various powers are vested in the hands of trustees, enabling them to raise £12,000 by a tax on vessels passing the bar [the large sandbank at the mouth of the Tawe]. Regular pilots have been appointed ... and a pier [breakwater] built on the western side of the river [which thrust straight out into Swanzey Bay], and another about built on the opposite side [from Salthouse Point it curved westwards to enclose Fabian's Bay], for the purpose of increasing the depth of water on the bar ... leaving only a passage between the' two breakwaters of approximately 70 metres.

Because ships often had to wait weeks for a cargo due to the difficulties of getting raw material such as coal to the quays, it became imperative that a canal should be built to link the Swansea Valley enterprises to the port. Work commenced in March 1793; it was a massive undertaking. According to the Revd. Oldisworth (1802), 'The course of the canal is from the [Cambrian] pottery, by Landore,

The Mumbles Lighthouse, built 1791-94, originally had two braziers, one above the other.
The grey, stone-built gun emplacement that surrounds the lighthouse on the south and east
was erected in 1860

Morriston, Clydach, Ynyspenllwch [near Clydach] and Ynyscedwyn to Hennoyadd in Breckonshire'. The canal was 15 miles long, having 36 locks and several aqueducts. In the Lower Swanzey Valley it incorporated the earlier canal built by Sir John Morris, which had subsequently been incorporated into the Trewyddfa Canal owned by the duke of Beaufort. Completed in December 1798, the Swanzey Canal was conveying up to 500,000 tons of material a year by the middle of the 19th century.

Towards the end of the 1700s a rapidly growing population caused a shortage of food which led to unrest across Britain. There were several instances in Swanzey in which workers showed their dissatisfaction, but one of the most serious occurrences took place in February 1793 when several hundred copper workers and colliers left Morriston to protest about the cost of essential foods and demand higher wages. As they marched towards Swanzey the protestors raided farms and work premises, calling upon others to join them. The authorities at Swanzey were already in a state of panic due to previous unrest and had sent for troops. The timely arrival of dragoons saved the town from being ransacked.

Britain was almost continuously at war with France during the period 1793 – 1813, and when 'three French frigates and a corvette' were seen 'hovering about off the Worm's Head', the portreeve wrote a letter, dated 22 February 1797 to the appropriate authorities, expressing concern that if 'a small (enemy) vessel … should come to the Mumbles (where there are frequently from sixty to one hundred sail … lying at anchor), [it could] very easily take and destroy the greater part of them and do other serious mischief'. The portreeve went on to suggest that if 'a dozen or fifteen long twelve or eighteen-pounders [were] sent down … with the necessary ammunition, they may be placed to' thwart any attack 'by the enemy'. He then drew attention to the fact 'that the Royal Swanzey Volunteers – consisting of

180 men – are stationed at Swanzey' with orders 'to exercise great guns … if any can be obtained'. Six years later two six-pounders were mounted on the headland, which the Corporation had to pay for, but it was not until 1860 that the stone-built gun emplacement fronting the now defunct Mumbles Lighthouse on its southern side was erected, costing the War Department a hefty £10,000.

Guns were not the only measures taken to defend Gower. Beacons were established at Oystermouth and on the eastern end of Cefn Bryn at a place that became known as the 'Beacons'. Ernest Helme of Hillend formed a troop of Yeomanry. Port Eynon was the headquarters of the blue-uniformed Sea Fencibles, armed with pikes and cutlasses. In 1798, Thomas Gordon of Llanrhidian was appointed captain of a company of the Glamorgan Rangers. There may have been a troop of Volunteer Cavalry based at Bishopston. All these units were militia, placed under the command of Lieutenant-Colonel Thomas Mansel Talbot. Neither Talbot nor his militia ever saw active service.

There is no record of Catholics in Gower from the time of the Reformation, but in 1797 Fr. Plowden, a Jesuit from Bristol, established a mission in the Plas, his reason for doing so being that Swanzey was 'a large trading town and much frequented by the Irish'. A purpose-built chapel was opened in 1812 by a Frenchman, Fr. Sejan, in Nelson Place, although his congregation appears to have numbered no more than a dozen adults. By 1838 there were 400 Catholics in Swanzey, most of them from Ireland. Their numbers rose sharply following the potato famine of 1845-47, so much so that within a few years the Greenhill district of Swanzey became known as 'Little Ireland'. For many Irish, Swanzey was no more than a place where they could earn their fare to America. They were not liked by the locals because of their willingness to work for lower wages, and in 1826 there was an instance in which Irish employees at a copper works were 'violently driven off' by non-Irish workers.

When the Swanzey-born poet, Dylan Thomas, spoke of his birthplace as an 'ugly, lovely town' he reiterated in three short words a difference of opinion that had existed for 200 years. There seems to have been, until recently, conflicting views as to whether the town should be a fashionable resort or a magnet for industry. In the late 18th to early 19th century, when books on travel were in vogue, many visitors to Swanzey wrote about what they saw. When H.P. Wyndham visited the town in 1774 he observed 'more miserable hovels than are to be found in the most indigent villages of England'. Thirteen years later, John Byng wrote of 'a nasty town' and complained of 'much bad pavement to our inn in High Street', which he described as 'very dirty and very dear'. What caught the eye of J. Manners (1795-97) was the 'columns of smoke which wound along the sides of the hills in spiral wreaths and filled the valley'. This smoke poisoned the western side of Kilvey Hill, a phenomenon that was apparent as early as 1802 when Oldisworth referred to 'a hill rendered barren by sulphurous influences of the neighbouring [White Rock] copper works at Foxhole'.

Yet there were those who saw Swanzey in an entirely different light. H. Skrine was amazed to find, in 1798, 'amidst the noise of manufactures ... all the resources of polished society'. The Revd. J. Evans remarked, in 1803, on 'the spaciousness of its streets, the appearance of the buildings'. In 1800, J. Skinner referred to the town 'as a bathing place' though 'by no means equal to Tenby', whereas in the opinion of E.D. Clarke (1798) it was 'almost equal to Weymouth with its white sand and beautiful shore'. Evans went one step further, declaring that Swanzey Bay was comparable 'the bay of Naples'. It comes as no surprise that, further west, Wigstead should declare, in 1797, that 'after passing along a rugged road, Caswell Bay opens, where there is the finest sandy beach I ever saw'. Yet Skrine saw the Gower peninsula as 'a rocky and uninteresting district except where the sea views enliven it ... a dreary and desolate wild far from the resorts of men'.

Most topographers travelled the hard way—on foot—as did the Revd. R. Warner in 1803 when, on his approach to Swanzey, he and his company 'judged it necessary to make as smart an appearance there as the situation of our wardrobes ... would allow; having therefore brushed up at a small village, about a mile from the town, and hired a lad to carry our knapsacks, we boldly proceeded to the Mackworth Arms'. That same year, J.T. Barber left Bristol to make his approach by sea, paying a half crown for a crossing that was made uncomfortable by wind and rain in a ship that had not been designed for carrying passengers. Both Warner and Barber explored the town and the Lower Swanzey Valley, but Barber proved to be the more adventurous, for after 'an excursion across the sands' of Swanzey Bay, he passed through 'the whitened town of Oystermouth' to brave the odds in the peninsula, which he found to be 'wild and dreary'.

Like Skrine five years earlier, Barber could not 'imagine what motive could induce' Mr. Talbot to live at Penrice on 'a bleak unfrequented coast'. After writing about Arthur's Stone on Cefn Bryn—which he described as ' a relic of the Druidical age', he felt obliged to comment on both Weobley Castle and Worm's Head, blaming his failure to view these places on 'difficulty of access and their out-of-the-way' locations. After hiring 'a poor little hack, at two guineas for a fortnight's use', he 'set forth over a high romantic district of Loughor, [then] a poor village; but still exhibiting the ruined keep of its castle, on a raised mound surrounded by a moat. From this place, soiled with filth of neighbouring collieries', he forded the estuary, a task which he described as 'by no means enviable; for, in addition to fording a rapid current over a rough stoney bottom, large hollows are formed by vessels at low water, which, not appearing, sometimes entrap the unsuspecting traveller, who may think himself well off if he escape with only a ducking'. He concluded that he and his companion had 'thanked our stars when we got across'.

When the Revd. J. Evans penned his *Letters* of 1803, he claimed it was the wish of many locals 'that Swanzey should be viewed in the light of a fashionable resort, rather than as a trading town', thereby cashing in on the belief that bathing in sea-water—even drinking it—was beneficial to health. Visitors came to Swanzey by scheduled coach, or left Bristol on the *Prince Royal* yacht which sailed twice weekly, 'wind and weather permitting'. The well-to-do invariably travelled in their own carriages and inns such as the Bush in High Street could accommodate up to ten carriages and provided 25 stalls for horses. The Mackworth Arms in Wind Street and the Cambrian Hotel on the Burrows were among the best inns in town, but most visitors preferred to stay in one of the 30 to 40 lodging houses, especially those on the Burrows which Evans described in 1803 as 'neat and pleasant, commanding a view of the river and bay.'

Bathing machines were available, described as 'similar to ... a coach ... the wheels high and strong ... In the front is a platform,' providing entry into 'a neat dressing room ... At the back opens a door, and, by means of a flight of steps ... the bathers descend into the water, concealed from public view by a large umbrella of canvas stretched on hoops'.

Evans complained that Swanzey did not have the amenities that were to be found at Weymouth, whereas Oldisworth in 1802 described a walk beside the Swanzey canal as 'very pleasing, affording many objects worth observation'. There was also the harbour to be viewed, trips to Oystermouth and Caswell Bay, and by 1823 boats were taking visitors to view the magnificent Gower coastline. To the east there was racing on the Crymlyn Burrows. There had been a theatre in Wind Street since 1785, but this was superseded by a larger one, sponsored by the gentry and built in Goat Street between 1806-07.

When writing of his travels in 1798 the Revd. R. Warner mentioned that there were 'two extensive breweries', in Swanzey, one of which, the Singleton Brewery, stood a little to the east of the present-day Grand Theatre, on the site of what was once the United Welsh bus garage. The brewery had been sited there because of the 'purity and sweetness' of a nearby spring. The establishment later became known as the Swanzey Old Brewery until its closure about 1930. The other brewery stood in the Strand near the bottom of King's Lane.

By 1800 the forests that had clothed Gower had all but gone; what woodland remained was confined to secluded valleys. In peninsula Gower (southwards of a line extending from Penclawdd to Brynmill) the English language ruled supreme, except for a sprinkling of Welsh on the north coast. Welsh remained the language of the northern hinterland (north of a line from Gorseinion to the parish church of St. Johns near Swanzey), the heartland of the language being the Tawe Valley and the remote yet partially industrialized parish of Llangwig where, from 1750 onwards, immigrants from all over South Wales had come in search of work. Between the two extremes the people of 'middle' Gower, including Swanzey, were bilingual. From 1800 onwards the number of English immigrants rose, coming mainly from the counties of Somerset, Gloucestershire, Devon and Cornwall. As already mentioned, they came from Ireland, too, though their numbers remained relatively small until after the potato famine of 1845-47.

The first census in the U.K., taken in 1801, records that the Town and Franchise of Swanzey had a population of 6,831, of which 1,196 were employed in

Regency houses, Cambrian Place,
built on the Little Burrows,
once the most fashionable quarter in Swansea

'trade, manufactures and handicrafts'. During the next 50 years, the business and commercial section of the town expanded westwards on the line of Oxford Street, whereas the most select quarters centred around Wind Street and the (little) Burrows to the south where, between 1770 and 1820, many fine Georgian and Regency houses were built, and where public buildings such as the Assembly Rooms (1811-21), the new Townhall (completed 1829) and the Royal Institute of South Wales (the Museum, in 1841) were built. The well-to-do industrialists and businessmen were also moving westwards, building a great many villas with spacious grounds along the lower slopes of Townhill (for example Windsor Lodge, Heathfield Lodge, Mansion House) all the way to the Uplands and

The Royal Institute of South Wales (the Museum), a two-storeyed building fronted by
Ionic columns, was completed in 1841

into the barony of Sketty, one of the most westerly mansions being Woodland which later became Clyne Castle.

There were many working-class houses in Swanzey and, according to Sophie Ward (1791) they were 'two-storyed high, covered with slate ... the fronts being white over ... generally having geraniums at their windows'. Ward's observations were confirmed by the three houses that, until 1954-55, had stood in Pottery Street, about 100 metres north of High Street Station. Built between 1813 and 1823, each of these houses had contained one room on both ground and first-floor level, each measuring little more than $4^1/_2$m square with a staircase opposite the front door. Each house had two sash windows at the front, one on each floor, and at the rear they had a door—but no windows—that led to a rear garden. A soakaway closet had been shared by the occupants of the three houses. Originally there had been 45 houses in Pottery Street, some of the roofs of which extended downwards at the rear to provide an extra room on the ground floor. It has been estimated that there had been about 1,000 of these houses in Swanzey by the mid-19th century. Houses of similar date, though somewhat larger, can be seen in Clifton Hill, the steep slope off Alexander Road, and in Pleasant Street.

Beyond the town the main concentration of working-class communities grew up to the north, skirting the west bank of the Tawe, from Vivian's Town (the Hafod) to Morriston; beyond Morriston, industrial communities such as Clydach and Pontardawe were to remain scattered, as did similar communities on the 'East Side' of the Tawe, from Port Tennant to Llansamlet. Other lines of expansion followed

Clifton Hill. These houses, built in 1813-23, are a survival of the oldest working-class houses in Swansea. Note the arched doorways, a feature of the time. A large proportion of the houses were smaller than the ones seen here, consisting of only two rooms, one on each floor

Remains of Vivian family's copper works
at the Hafod

the Llangyfelach and Carmarthen roads. Less extensive industrial communities, all of them scattered, also became established on the east bank of the River Loughor, from Penclawdd to Pontardulais. Elsewhere Gower remained essentially rural, despite the limestone quarries and the woollen mills that studded the peninsula.

Among the many industrial dynasties to establish themselves in and around Swansea the greatest of them all was the Vivians. The founder of this dynasty, John Vivian of Truro in Cornwall, came to Gower shortly after 1800 to take up a temporary partnership in the copper smelting works at Penclawdd, but it was not until 1810, when he established his own copper works at the Hafod, that he began to prosper. When he died in 1826 his second son, John Henry Vivian, expanded the family business—Vivian and Sons—by involving himself in numerous enterprises, including coalmining and shipping, becoming immensely wealthy and influential. While he lived in luxury on the open spaces west of the town, the area around his Hafod copper works became known as Vivian's Town (now the Hafod district), which was described in 1840 as 'serried rows of back-to-back houses that eat their way through hedge and field, to climb and spread as best they may, unpleasant, throughout the Vale. Hastily built, ugly, unsanitary and overcrowded, these were the homes' of his workmen and their families'.

After marrying the beautiful Sarah Jones in 1816, John Henry took up residence in an octagonally-shaped mansion called Marino, which he soon enlarged to become 'one of the finest residences in the county'. Not content with this he then converted the mansion into the magnificent Singleton Abbey (now part of the University College), leaving Sarah—who bore nine children—to create luxurious gardens around the house. Apart from building the Swiss Cottage that still stands in Singleton Park, John Henry bought Parc Wern (now Parc Beck) as a dower house for Sarah. Unfortunately, when he died in 1855, Sarah refused to leave Singleton Abbey and her eldest son, Henry Hussy—who should have taken over the house—was obliged to reside at Park Wern until she died in 1886.

The Dillwyns were as well known as the Vivians. The family connection with Gower began in 1801-02 when William Dillwyn, a London quaker and successful

Singleton Abbey, home of J.H. Vivian; now part of the University

businessman, bought the Cambrian Pottery for his son, Lewis Weston Dillwyn, who was more interested in botany and conchology, and who became the author of several scientific books. In 1807, Lewis married Mary Adams, the illegitimate daughter of Colonel John Llywelyn, a wealthy Glamorgan landowner. Ten years later, when the colonel died, Lewis became a trustee for his eldest son, John, heir to the Llywelyn estate of Penllergaer and other estates in the eastern part of Glamorgan. In 1832 Lewis became one of two M.P.s elected to represent Glamorgan after the Reform Act.

John—who became known as John Dillwyn Llywelyn—took possession of his inheritance in 1831. John was no businessman, preferring to pursue his interest in photography and science, confident that his wealth would support him. He married into the Talbot family and his main residence was at Penllergaer, demolished in 1961 to make way for the Lliw Valley District Council offices. His younger brother, Lewis Llywelyn Dillwyn, did not have the benefit of a vast inheritance, but managed the Cambrian Pottery until such time as he sold it to build the magnificent Henrefoilan House (now owned by the University Collage). Lewis made a name for himself as a radical M.P., representing Swanzey for several decades from 1855 onwards.

Swiss Cottage, Singleton Park, built by J.H. Vivian

In August 1802, Lord Horatio Nelson and the Hamiltons came to Swanzey for a few days, staying at the Mackworth Arms and at Worcester Place which, according to Oldisworth, 'consists of a range of neat houses, the chief of which is the residence of Thomas Morgan, Esq., the present portreeve, and proprietor of the whole row'. Morgan had obtained a lease from the duke of Beaufort in 1790 for the land north of the 1774 market, where he demolished all trace of the 'old' castle, and built seven houses, the largest of which he called Worcester Place House in honour of the duke who still held the title of earl of Worcester. The house, which overlooked the Strand, had a large Georgian bow window and survived until it was destroyed in an air raid in February 1941.

No-one can say how many pits were in Gower at any given time, but in his *Letters* of 1803, Evans claimed that 'The largest colliery is at Pentre, the property of Mr.

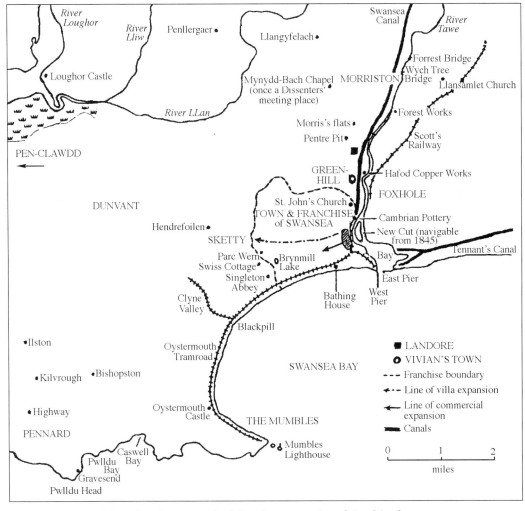

Map showing several of the places mentioned in this chapter

Morris of Clasemont (grandson of the first John Morris). The whole hill is full of coal … obtained by what the miners term open adits, i.e., horizontal shafts driven into the hill, which forms levels for draining the work as well as ways for the delivery of the coal. There are within some vertical shafts beneath these levels … One of the adits, which we traced about a mile in length, admits low wagons, holding a chaldron each, which running on an iron railway, one horse with ease delivers at the (Landore) quay'. Evans also gave figures taken from the 'the Custom House', which recorded that 'The number of vessels that cleared out (of Swanzey) in 1768 was 694, consisting of 30,681 tons; in 1798, 2,021, consisting of 120,713 tons; and in 1800, the supposed number was 3,000, consisting of about 200,000 tons. The trade is principally with London, the coasts of Devon and Cornwall, Bristol, Ireland and the Baltic'.

The year 1804 is significant in that it saw the establishment of a local news-paper, the *Cambrian*, which spelt the town's name as Swansea, a spelling that has persisted to this day. The same year the earliest recorded auction known as 'tick-eting' took place, the agents of the copper smelters gathering at the Mackworth Arms to present 'tickets' stating their offering price for 'parcels' of ore, which were sold to the highest bidder. The practice persisted intermittently until the middle of the 19th century.

According to an old chart of Swansea Bay, there had been a quay at Blackpill for the purpose of shipping coal and other materials from Clyne Valley Woods. The chart also showed that there had been a track across the sands linking Swansea to Mumbles. On 4 July 1804 a meeting took place at the Bush Hotel, High Street, in which Sir John Morris addressed for the first time members of the newly-formed Oystermouth Railway or Tramroad Company. In August that year the first tracks were laid for a line on which single horse-drawn wagons could convey limestone and iron from the Mumbles along the sea front to where the museum now stands, and continue up the Strand to link up with the Swansea Canal near the Cambrian Pottery. There were to be two branch lines, one from Blackpill to Morris's mines in the Clyne Valley, and one from near the bottom of Wind Street to the western pier. The line opened in the spring of 1806, and on 25 March the following year the world's first passenger rail service came into existence. In a letter dated 1808, a visitor, Elizabeth Spence, gave an account of her journey to Oystermouth: I was conveyed there in a carriage of a singular construction, built for the convenience of parties, who go hence to Oystermouth to spend the day. This car contains twelve persons and is constructed chiefly of iron, its four wheels run on an iron railway by the aid of one horse, and is an easy and light vehicle'.

The passenger service continued until 1826 (reopening in 1860) when a turn-pike road from Swansea to Mumbles offered alternative means of travel. By then there were a number of turnpike roads radiating from Swansea, with chains or gates at sites that had formerly been occupied by the gates in the town wall. A mile or two further out the town was surrounded by a second ring of chains or gates—near St. Helen's cricket ground, at Sketty Cross, Cwmbwrla and the Hafod—and an outer

Mumbles Railway, as painted by J. Ashford in 1819. The line was opened in 1806 and the passenger service followed a year later

ring arced from Loughor to the Wychtree Bridge at Morriston. This system of levying tolls for the improvement of roads continued to exist until, with the establishment of the Roads Board in 1844, they were phased out over a period of 30 years.

In 1805 the *Cambrian* recorded how a customs officer, George Beynon, with the aid of Sea Fencibles, had descended on Rhosili sands and driven off a gang of smugglers, seizing no less than 100 casks of spirits and wine. Smuggling activity is known to have taken place in Gower as early as the 16th century, but during the 18th century it was pursued on an unprecedented scale due to the amount of duty levied on commodities such as tea, tobacco, brandy and lace, some of which were taxed as much as seven times their marketable value. Gower, being remote and with its southern coastline studded with secluded bays, was ideally situated for the organized gangs which operated in the area. Ships, usually of French origin, were directed to a beach under cover of darkness using lanterns, where farm labourers and quarrymen were waiting to carry the contraband inland and hide it in homes and haystacks. Spirits came in three to four gallon casks and, with the aid of cordage, a man could carry two such casks, one at his chest, one at his back. No one knows the true extent of this activity as the records only refer to the occasional success of the excisemen, but a report compiled in August 1795 estimated that 'at least 5,000 kegs of liquor had been landed [in Gower] within … six months [and that] all the vessels from Ireland that come for coals … bring soap or salt in great quantities'.

At Port Eynon during the 18th century, where there were plenty of oystermen and quarrymen only too willing to supplement their meagre wages, there were up to eight excisemen stationed in the village, having use of a boat and a watch-house on Port Eynon Point—not that the king's officers had things all their own way: there were too many bays and there was always the risk that the smugglers could turn nasty, as happened in March 1805 when officers William Webb and Thomas Seward were set upon to the extent that Seward had to limp home and Webb, who was wounded, was locked up in a cottage while the smugglers got on with their work. Perhaps the excisemen's greatest triumph—or near failure—occurred in April 1803 when Francis Bevan seized 420 casks at Highway in the parish of Pennard. The casks were loaded onto wagons, destined for Swansea, and throughout the journey a mob of 200 intoxicated men and women harried the wagon train all the way to Wind Street. From a detailed report of the incident there can be little doubt that the drivers, along with their escort of 50 Sea Fencibles, were no less intoxicated than the mob. Smugglers continued to make use of Gower until, in 1822, the Royal Navy began blockading the Bristol Channel.

An Act of Parliament in 1809 led to the creation in Swansea of Paving Commissioners made up of volunteers and councillors, whose ultimate responsibilities were watches, fire-fighting, street-lighting, street-cleansing, paving, drainage and the public slaughterhouse. When the Swansea Gas Company was formed a few years later a gas works was built at Dyfatty, street lamps were set up and the lights came on in 1821. By 1848 there were 183 street lamps in the town. Between 1821 and 1823 the main streets were re-laid, 'on each side of which, a wide flagging … was carried close to the walls' of houses. By 1845 there were eight men and four carts employed to clean the streets, but attempts to provide better drainage were totally inadequate. This was to prove disastrous in a rapidly expanding town where the only source of drinking water were the numerous springs and wells that were to be found in and around the town. In many places the contents of soak-away privies percolated through the soil to contaminate the water of wells and springs.

The Assembly Rooms, Cambrian Place, built 1811-21, was where the affluent met socially. The building has recently been converted into flats

No town could be without assembly rooms, a place where the affluent could converse, dance or play cards. The Mackworth

Arms, described by the Revd. R. Warner in 1798 as 'the best inn in' Swansea, provided such amenities as early as 1776. The Assembly Rooms that were built on the Burrows between 1811 and 1821 (recently converted into a block of flats) were described by the *Cambrian* as comprising of 'a Commercial-Room, Library, Ball-Room, Supper-Room, Card-Room, Billiard-Room, Bar, Kitchen and Pantries'. These rooms were intended to delight both visitors and the local gentry for many years to come. Unfortunately, by 1840 the Burrows days as the most fashionable place in town were numbered—industry, the construction of docks and a need for more working class houses all conspired to bring about its decline.

About 1808 a voluntary dispensary had been established at Swansea and, in 1817, it was moved to larger premises, occupying the eastern part of a disused bathing house about a half a mile from the town, somewhere in the vicinity of

A post card showing the various markets that have existed in Swansea.
Top left: The market built in 1774 occupied the 'new' castle courtyard
and part of Worcester Place to the north.
Top right: The market built in 1897.
Bottom right: Cromwellian Market as painted by Calvert Richard Jones in 1839,
which he did in part from memory. It portrays a much quieter scene than the one portrayed
by John Nixon in 1799 (for which see p.130).
Bottom left: The first Oxford Street Market as it appeared in 1862. The row of chimneys
on the right belong to the butchers' stalls that lined the north side of what basically is an
open-air market, in the centre of which stood the clocktower in the circular picture

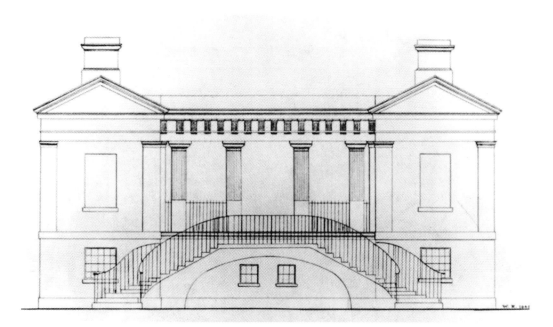

First Town Hall in Somerset Place completed in 1829

today's County Hall. The premises proved large enough to open an infirmary, one that could receive 16 inpatients. That same year (1817) the western half of the building was converted for use as a House of Correction, or workhouse, as the castle premises were no longer suitable for housing 180 inmates.

In the early 1820s, George Tennant took over an existing canal (established in 1790) in the Neath area and began extending it through the Crymlyn Bog to the east side of Fabian's Bay. When it opened in May 1824 the Tennant Canal enabled Neath industrialists to benefit from the better port facilities in the area that later became known as Port Tennant.

A descendant of a cadet branch of the Penreses, Major Thomas Penrice of Great Yarmouth, came to Gower in 1820 and purchased Kilvrough Manor (built by a descendant of Rowland Dawkin) and its demesne. Eight years later, Penrice exchanged property in Northamptonshire for all the possessions in Gower of All Souls Collage, Oxford. A veteran lancer of the Peninsular War, the major took command of the Swansea and Fairwood Corps of Yeoman Cavalry, a militia unit numbering around 160 men. On the 3 June 1831 he was ordered to muster and march to Merthyr to quell the riots there. When he arrived on the outskirts of the town with an advance party of 30 men, he was surrounded and his men disarmed by a starving mob of thousands. The incident led to the disbanding of the corps, much to the annoyance of the major. When he died in 1845, his estate, which passed to his nephew and namesake, was, within Gower, second in size only to that of the Talbots, amounting to several thousand acres. The estate then passed to the nephew's daughter, and so the Penrice bid to return to former glory proved short lived. Kilvrough Manor is now a holiday and education centre for young people.

Due to the failure of the 1774 market and the worsening congestion around Island House, the Swansea Corporation obtained an Act of Parliament in 1828, empowering it to erect 'a new market for corn, cattle, horses, sheep, butchers' meat, poultry and other marketable commodities', and for that purpose Calvert Richard Jones, a prominent burgess who had been portreeve in 1823-24, gifted the Corporation a two-acre site adjoining Oxford Street known as the Ropewalk Field. The first Oxford Street market opened on 25 September 1830; it consisted of pent-house stalls around the perimeter of what was basically an open-air site; in all there were 89 stalls. A market house, incorporating a committee room, weighing room and a clock tower, stood in the centre of the market.

The old Townhall in front of the castle ceased to be used as such when, in October 1829, a new building in Somerset Place was completed. The new Townhall—known as the Guildhall—no longer exists, being replaced by a later, modified building on the same site that also became known as the Guildhall (now the Dylan Thomas Centre). The old Townhall continued in use as a police station and a police court until a purpose-built premises became available in Goat Street in 1845. The old Townhall was then taken over by the First Glamorgan Artillery Volunteers and finally demolished in 1856.

The census of 1831 records that:

Llangyfelach Hundred had a population of 12,787
                there were 2,489 families
                of which 1,353 were engaged mainly if trade manufactures & handicraft
                        676 in agriculture
                        503 in unspecified employment

Swansea Hundred had a population of 10,709 (not including Swansea)
                there were 2,252 families
                of which 465 were engaged mainly in trade manufactures & handicraft
                        971 in agriculture
                        816 in unspecified employment

Town & Franchise of Swansea had	13,694 persons residing there
there were	2,955 families
of which	1,289 were engaged mainly in trade manufactures & handicraft
	33 in agriculture
	1,633 in unspecified employment
Total population of Gower	37,190

The Reform Act of 1832 allocated Glamorgan a second county M.P., the first man to represent the western half of the county being a Liberal, C.R.M. Talbot of Margam, who held the seat until 1890. Swansea also acquired its own M.P., but the burgesses had to share their voting with the burgesses of Loughor, Neath, Aberavon and Kenfig. There were changes, too, in the voting area of Swansea. The old Town and Franchise had contained 1,918 acres; this was expanded to 5,363 acres by the addition of the hamlet of St. Thomas, the parish of St. John and portions of the parishes of Llangyfelach and Llansamlet. The new voting area became known as the Parliamentary Borough of Swansea. The first man to represent Swansea and its four contributory boroughs—a constituency known as Swansea and District—was yet another Liberal, J.H. Vivian, who held the seat until his death in 1855.

The Reform Bill had been the cause of political unrest for over a year prior to it being passed in May 1832. Against a background of issues such as slavery, emancipation of Jews and Catholics, the injustices of Corn, Poor and Game Laws there had been serious working class riots such as the one that had led to the disbandment of Major Penrice's yeoman cavalry. Even demands for the right to vote by middle class entrepreneurs were seen as a threat to the age-old privileges of the landed gentry and burgesses. In short, revolution was in the air—but no matter how hotly the issues had been debated in Swansea they became secondary to the concern expressed about a cholera epidemic that broke out between July and September and did not die down until October. In all there were 423 cases reported and 148 people died. The worst affected area was the lower town, in particular Little Wind Street, Frog Street, Pig Street, Butter Street and the Strand. An inadequate water supply and an ineffective drainage system were blamed for the epidemic. When cholera visited Swansea again 17 years later, the lower part of the town escaped another round of horrors due to a 'plentiful supply of fresh water' provided by the Swansea Waterworks Company from the reservoir that had been constructed at Brynmill (now the lake in Brynmill Park) in 1837.

The Municipal Corporations Act of 1835 resulted in Swansea becoming a municipal borough, its boundaries coinciding with those of the Parliamentary Borough; this would appear to have almost doubled the borough's population, for in the 1841 census the population of the Town and Franchise stood at 16,787 persons, whereas the figure given for the municipal borough was 31,461 persons. There were two wards—North and South—for the election of 24 councillors, six of whom were aldermen. The office of portreeve became defunct, replaced by that of mayor—a council chairman no longer selected by the steward, but elected by members of the council. In short, the duke of Beaufort could no longer consider Swansea as 'my borough', his steward no longer controlled the town, and the first mayor was Nathaniel Cameron. Another significant change was that the burgesses, who then numbered 104 men, were no longer the élite, for franchise was given to all male householders who contributed towards the poor rate.

Conclusion

Despite periodic depressions the Tawe Valley continued to expand in the field of extractive industries, the predominance of copper giving way to steel and tinplate, although coalmining still reigned supreme until decline followed the First World War. The Valley's industrial expansion had been made possible by Swansea's development as a port. The most significant step in the construction of docks was the diversion of the Tawe (between the Cambrian Pottery and the ancient ferry) to its present position further east; known as the New Cut, it became navigable in 1845. What had been a bend in the river close to the Strand was converted into the North Dock, equipped with lock gates, which opened in 1852. The South Dock opened in 1859, and by 1920 the whole of Fabian's Bay had been transformed into docks. The

Swansea Marina

extractive industries are now a thing of the past, the majority of people today, in both Swansea and the Tawe Valley, being employed in the service industry. The only dock that has not been filled in, or does not face an uncertain future, is the South Dock which has been converted into a marina, surrounded by a residential area and by a leisure complex. The town has expanded well beyond its municipal boundaries of 1835, the number of houses within its bounds multiplying from 3,369 in 1845 to around 50,000 in 1970, a quarter of which were built by the local councils.

The industrialization that had taken root around the Loughor estuary (between Penclawdd and Pontardulais) has gone, and the inland massif between the Tawe and Loughor rivers has lost its woodland and its upland farms, to become windswept moorland, home for sheep. That is not to say the northern hinterland has nothing to offer the adventurous motorist or the intrepid walker, whilst Swansea has much to offer both locals and visitors alike, but the jewel in the crown is peninsula Gower, little affected by industrialization and, therefore, still essentially rural in character. Since the Second World War the peninsula has been colonized by higher-income commuters and, seasonally, by holiday-makers; this is partly because it is Britain's prime area of outstanding natural beauty, and also because it is a place where much of its past can still be seen in the landscape—everything from prehistoric tombs to 19th-century mansions.

References

Chapter II

1. Although condensed, what has been said of Gruffudd ap Rhys comes from the *Brut y Tywysogion*—the Chronicle of the Princes (of Wales)—of which there are three main versions. One of them, the Gwentian version, otherwise known as the *Book of Aberpergwm*, is the fanciful but fraudulent work of Iolo Morgannwg, a 19th-century antiquarian, and can, therefore, be dismissed.

Chapter IV

1. A copy of the charter was found in a collection of papers known as the *Breviate of Domesday* originally kept at Margam Abbey to which de Breos and his descendants were patrons. Attached to the charter, and probably written many years later in Norman-French, is a description of the boundaries as they may have been about 1300.

Chapter V

1. The earliest description of Gower is to be found in the *Breviate of Domesday*, attached to a copy of King John's charter of 1203 (see pp.45-46). The document in question is dated to around 1300, which suggests that, at the time, William's son still considered the disputed territory to be his.

2. John de Breos had seized the manor in 1229 under similar circumstances.

3. In the charter to the men of Gower it is *Kylthywasta*, possibly the 'waste of Killay Common', or it could refer to *Gellywasted* about a 2 miles to the north-east of Llangyfelach Church.

Chapter VII

1. There are those who believe that the town house was situated just outside the outer bailey, 'next to the bridge of the fortress' on the south side and, therefore, adjoining 'the street called the Market Place', which was a square at the top of what is now Wind Street.

2. Born in 1618, the son of David Johnes, Philip Jones claimed descent from Gruffydd ap Cadifor of early 13th-century fame. He is often described as a free-

holder whose birthplace had been the family farm of Pen y waun near Llangyfelach Church, but in a letter written in 1755 by Mary Edwin, the wife of one of his descendants, it states that he was born in Swanzey, in the Great House that had belonged to his father and grandfather before him. Situated in the *upper town* of Swanzey, 'above the [north] gate' at the upper angle of the present-day High Street and King's Lane, the Great House was described by Mary Edwin as one of the better class of properties in the town, having thick walls, huge chimneys, high-pitched gables, dormer windows and a spacious garden that sloped to the strand. The house was pulled down about 1750. At an unknown date, Jones married Jane, daughter of William Price of Gellihir, who had issue four sons and five daughters.

Bibliography

Chapter One

Tacitus, *Annals*, X11, 31-40; XV1, 29-39; Agricola, 14-17. For a modern account see V.E. Nash-Williams, *The Roman Frontier in Wales* (2nd edn., revised by M.G. Jarret 1969).

Antonine Itinerary of *c*.A.D. 300. For a modern account see A.L.F. Rivet *The British Section of the Antonine Itinerary, Britannic, 1* (1970)

Chapter Two

Nennius, *Historia Brittonum*. For a modern account see A.W. Wade-Evans *Nenius's History of the Britons* (1938)

W.J. Rees, *The Liber Landavensis* (The Book of Llandaff)

Annales Cambriae, ed. John Williams ab Ithel (Rerum Britannicorum medii aevi Scriptores; Rolls Series), (London 1858)

Geraldus Cambrensis (Gerald of Wales), *The Itinerary through Wales & The Description of Wales* as translated by Sir Richard Colt Hoare; also an abridged version by A.G. Prys-Jones (first published in 1955)

Rice Merrick, *Morganiae Archaiographia* of *c*.1578, ed. Brian Ll. James (1983)

Excavation at Castle Tower, Penmaen, by Prof. L. Alcock, *Ant. Journ.*, XLVl (1966), pp.178-210

Brut y Tywysogion, Red Book of Hergist Version, ed. and trans. by T. Jones (1955)

Brut y Tywysogion, Peniarth ms 20, trans. by T. Jones (Cardiff 1952)

Chapter Three

The *Brut* (both versions), *ibid.*

Florence of Worcester, *Gesta Stephani,* Book 1 (Forrester's translation), ed. by K.R. Potter (1955)

Gerald of Wales, *ibid.*

Annales, ibid.

Chapter Four

Breviate of Domesday

Annals de Margam

Chapter Five

The *Brut, ibid.*

J.G. Wood, *The Principal Rivers of Wales* (1811)

Edward Lluyd, *Parochialia*, 3 parts, Arch. Camb. Supplements, 1909-11, ed. R.H. Morris

Annales, ibid.

Breviate of Domesday,

Penrice and Margam, manuscript collection, National Library of Wales. Much of this material can be found in the Revd. J.D. Davies's *History of West Gower* (1877-94)

Black Book of St. Davids, compiled in 1326. For a full account of the two Gower manors see W.H. Jones, *History of Swansea and the Lordship of Gower,* pp 343-5

Chapter Six

John Leland *The Itinerary in Wales in or about the years 1536-9* ed. L.Toulmin-Smith (1906)

Black Book, ibid.

Annals of Owain Glyn Dwr. For a modern account see R.R. Davies *The Revolt of Owain Glyn Dwr* (Oxford University Press 1995); for a full account with respect to Gower see W.H. Jones, *History of Swansea and the Lordship of Gower,* Vol ll (Swansea 1992)

Chapter Seven

Leland Itinerary, ibid.

Common Hall Book and Book of Orders 1547-1665. Housed at University Collage, Swansea

Merrick, *Archaiographia, ibid.*

Hall Day Minute Book. Housed at University Collage, Swansea

G.G. Francis, *Charters Granted to the Chief Borough of Swansea* (1867, 1871)

Chapter Eight

Thomas Dineley, *An Account of the Progress of His Grace Henry the first Duke of Beaufort Through Wales, 1684,* ed. By R.W. Banks (1888)

Daniel Defoe, *A Tour of England and Wales* (1722)

Henry Skrine, *Two Successive Tours Throughout the Whole of Wales* (1798)

Revd. J.P. Oldisworth, *The Swansea Guide* of 1802

Revd. John Evans, *Letters Written During A Tour Through South Wales, in the year 1803*

Index

INDEX

INDEX

Wallicana 14, 20, 22
   Subboscus 22-23
   Supraboscus 22-23, 63, 64, 74, 81
Walter, Herbert 41
Walterston 19, 35, 110
Warner, Revd. R. 134
Warwick, William, earl of 19
   (*see also* Newburgh)
Waterton, de, Sir Hugh 83, 84, 85
Webb, William 143
Welsh, the 11-12, 40
Weobley 14, 69, 81, 86
   Castle 62, 69, *69*
Wesley, John 126
West Country links 121
West Pilton 19
Weston, de, Robert 81

Westown, manor of, in Llangenydd 109
William Rufus, King 10
Wilmott, Robert 117
Woodville, Elizabeth 88
wolves 5
Worm's Head **2**
Wyndham, H.P. 133

Y Faerdref, Clydach 21
Ye Goedre, nr. Hendrefoilan 88
Yniscedwyn 54, 121
Ynyspenllwch 121
Ystrad Ewias 28
   Tywi 9, 10, 35, 53

zinc works 129